# The Wit and Wisdom of
# Ozzie Guillen

## Brett Ballantini

### TRIUMPH
**B O O K S**

CHICAGO

This book is available in quantity at special discounts for your group or organization. For further information, contact:

Triumph Books
542 South Dearborn Street
Suite 750
Chicago, Illinois 60605
(312) 939-3330
Fax (312) 663-3557

Printed in U.S.A.
ISBN-13: 978-1-57243-867-5
ISBN-10: 1-57243-867-3
Design by Patricia Frey

*To the 2005 World Champion Chicago White Sox—*
*You will never truly know the gift you have given us all*

*To Angel, the love of my life—*
*You will never truly know the gift you are to me*

# Contents

Preface                                            vii

Acknowledgments                                     ix

Introduction                                        xi

1. Ozzie the Player                                  1

2. The New Hire                                      9

3. A Rocky Rookie Year                             13

4. Homeland: Venezuela                             19

5. Crosstown Comments                              27

6. 2005: Wire to Wire                              31

7. The Importance of Family                        41

8. A Division Series Sweep                         43

9. Jerry and Kenny                                 51

10. The White Sox Win the Pennant!                 59

11. Inside the Clubhouse                            67

12. A Historic World Series                         83

13. Aftermath/Looking Ahead                         93

Appendix                                           97

Notes                                             109

# Preface

It's true that Ozzie and I had a heated discussion when he interviewed with me for the White Sox manager's job after the 2003 season. And sure, it impressed me that he had the courage to stand up for himself and fight for what he believed in.

But that gives the impression that any Tom, Dick, or Harry can walk into my office, start jawing with me, and be handed a job. Not so.

What I value most in Ozzie is his honesty. What he says may make you mad, or make you think, or make you laugh—or sometimes, all three at once. But to me, it's refreshing. I deal with people straight on as well, and perhaps that's why Ozzie and I are so close.

The two of us are the same age, grew up playing for the same team, and have faced some of the same obstacles. Some say we are like brothers, and I won't dispute that except to say that I can't imagine any brother of mine talking as much as Ozzie does. But it's true that we have done a lot to make the White Sox a family, and I'm proud of the role both Ozzie and I have had in that.

I can still remember when Ozzie came and broke the news to me that I had been traded by the White Sox. He had tears in his eyes—and a few choice words for those in the organization who had lost faith in me. Typical Ozzie, and God bless him for it.

I hoped then that the next time we might shed tears together would be under better circumstances. Last October, that wish came true with our World Series win, and I believe now what I believed when I hired Ozzie: I couldn't have picked a better guy to succeed with.

—Kenny Williams

# Acknowledgments

I am indebted to Scott Reifert of the Chicago White Sox for his assistance over the course of the 2005 season. To list all of his kindnesses would extend this work far too long, but suffice it to say that, like a great player on the field, Scott knows just where to be and when. He has a great connection to the "real" fan and does the White Sox organization proud. Additional thanks are due to my compadres in the White Sox communications department, Amy Kress, Katie Kirby, and Nicole Crudo.

Thanks also go to the White Sox coaching staff and roster for their assistance in compiling this book, particularly Frank Thomas, Jermaine Dye, Don Cooper, Tadahito Iguchi, Mark Buehrle, Paul Konerko, Joe Crede, A. J. Pierzynski, Orlando Hernandez, and Jose Contreras.

Kenny Williams was generous with his time and attention, as was Ozzie Guillen himself. Here's a toast to the architects of the White Sox title season.

My wife, Angelique, was 14–1 on the season at U.S. Cellular Field and is at least as responsible for the World Series win as Jerry Reinsdorf's John Wayne statue. Thanks also to my dad, Larry, for all the balls we've tossed in Armour Park, my mother, Carole, for helping us through

Orlando Hernandez's sixth inning in Boston, and my sister, Beth, for keeping the faith through countless phone call updates from down south.

# Introduction

The day I met Ozzie Guillen, he was sitting in the White Sox dugout at U.S. Cellular Field. Wait, no, he was outside of the cage during batting practice, taunting an opposing player taking his BP. Well, maybe I was sprinting after him as he bounded across the field to disrupt infield practice.

Actually, he was probably doing all of the above. Ozzie has an energy that is difficult to harness and impossible to measure, which is no surprise to anyone who followed the 2005 White Sox with any interest.

The team's transformation under Ozzie was extraordinary. While the expectations of longtime White Sox fans were raised by Guillen's hiring in 2003, I don't think even *el presidente* of the Ozzie Guillen Fan Club would have imagined a World Series title in just two seasons.

But what was more endearing about Ozzie—and it's hard to find anything out there more endearing than wins—is the joy with which he plays the game. The energy that sent him bounding back and forth across the field on the day we first met is something that infects fans, players, and managers, at home and away.

Ozzie is first and foremost a baseball fan, and who can't appreciate him on that level?

Without even my asking, one of the first things Ozzie shared with me was his vision of the future. In that future, the White Sox have won the World Series, and he will hand the World Series trophy to the man he so dearly loves, his boss, White Sox owner Jerry Reinsdorf. All the fans in the stands, his "30,000 managers" who either cheer his every move or shout their criticisms to him in the dugout, are joyous beyond belief. Ozzie's vision vindicates Reinsdorf, GM Kenny Williams, Frank Thomas, and all the White Sox who fell short of a World Series.

Most of all, Ozzie wants the White Sox to be known, once and forever, as World Champions. Long after they forget his name, Guillen says, his imagined World Series title will remain.

He seems like a prophet now, his vision realized more fully than even he could have hoped. It couldn't have happened to a better guy—White Sox to the core.

Over the course of Chicago's triumphant 2005 season, Ozzie indeed became known as a prophet—but often, a kooky, deranged one. Before the season, he cussed out free agent turncoat Magglio Ordonez and chided his departed outfielder Carlos Lee. As the team's fortunes burgeoned during the season, Guillen threatened to retire—or, alternately, to manage for 30 more years. He taunted his own club in the middle of a pennant race with the infamous "We stink," mocked Wrigley Field, mourned a national hero, and had dustups with his own reliever, the enigmatic Damaso Marte.

Not many managers—surely not managers just into their forties—could inspire a book dedicated to documenting their quips and quotes. But Ozzie, on nearly every level, is no normal manager. Read on, and you're sure to find out why.

## chapter 1

# Ozzie the Player

O zzie Guillen was born in Venezuela, the wellspring of great defensive shortstops. In fact, Guillen was tutored by Ernesto Aparicio, uncle of White Sox Hall of Fame player Luis Aparicio—himself mentored by the first great Latin major leaguer, White Sox shortstop Chico Carrasquel.

In spite of such a lineage working for him, Guillen joined the White Sox in a most controversial manner. On December 6, 1984, the White Sox traded La Marr Hoyt, a hero of Chicago's recent playoff team and 1983 American League Cy Young Award winner, for the largely unknown Guillen. At the time, Guillen had been a success at the minor league level but had yet to play a major league game.

Chicago general manager Roland Hemond was skewered over the deal; the 29-year-old Hoyt was seen as having hundreds of great innings left in his arm, an ace who couldn't be shuttled away for a kid, no matter how promising. Even the legendary baseball writer Jerome Holtzman speculated that the trade was little more than a dump of Hoyt's $900,000 annual salary.

Today, the deal is considered one of the best in White Sox history.

Jerry Krause—later to achieve fame as the architect of the Chicago Bulls' six titles in the 1990s—was the source of Hemond's confidence in the trade. Krause's roots were as a baseball scout, and he had watched Guillen play in a dozen or so games in Triple A.

**Hemond:** There's a lot of satisfaction for me. Even though it's nearly 21 years later, it's nice to know one of your contributions to this current team results from that trade.

**Krause:** I wrote, "He's as smart a young player as I've ever seen."

**Hemond:** There was a lot of criticism here. Luckily, I was quickly vindicated when people saw Ozzie play.

**Krause:** There was a question about his arm. But I always noticed that he threw out the fast guys by a step, and the slow guys by a step. He wasn't going to waste that arm. He was just so bright.

Krause was sold on Guillen once he noticed that at every game, the first player out of the dugout was the skinny shortstop from Venezuela, who would study his opponents as they took batting practice.

While it is well known that Krause brought out the antagonistic side of many of his Bulls players, Guillen always accorded him with respect and appreciation, because it was Krause who was responsible for his opportunity with the White Sox. There was a special request, in fact, from Guillen on the day he was hired as White Sox manager.

**Krause:** Reinsdorf told me, "You have an invitation to a press conference on Monday. The new manager of the White Sox asks that you be there." Ozzie never forgot to this day.

**Hemond:** I remember being told [at the time of the trade] that he was a manager on the field, but [his 2005 success] goes beyond my wildest expectations. It's just so thrilling to see.[1]

Ozzie made the deal a steal for the White Sox right away; the 21-year-old won the American League Rookie of the Year handily, while Hoyt would win a mere 24 games in the rest of his career. Guillen's 12 errors led all AL shortstops in fielding, and his bat, considered to be merely a bonus, cut up pitchers to the tune of .273.

Guillen's range and acrobatics on defense earned comparisons to countryman forebears Luis Aparicio and Dave Concepcion, as well as his premier defensive contemporary and fellow Ozzie, Ozzie Smith.

The young shortstop's best asset of many was his feistiness, and beyond that he immediately won over fans with his skill, smile, and hustle. In an August 2, 1985, game, Guillen scored

Ozzie as a rookie in 1985

Ozzie stroking a single against the Tigers in 1996

from second on an infield hit in the eleventh, giving the White Sox a 6–5 win vs. the New York Yankees.

He played in All-Star Games in 1988, 1990, and 1991, and won a Gold Glove in 1990. On April 21, 1992, Guillen was lost for the season after a violent collision in short left field with Tim Raines (now Guillen's first-base coach). While he bounced back and recorded the two best batting averages of his career in the next two seasons, .280 and .288, his speed was largely eroded by the injury.

Guillen was a notorious free swinger, liable to take a cut at a ball on the ground and over his head in the course of the same at-bat. He set a major league record in 1996 with only 10 walks in 150 games, and his on-base percentage ranged from .265 to .325 over the course of his career. He never drew more than 26 walks in a single season.

On the plus side, Guillen consistently finished in the AL top 10 in triples, sacrifices, and fewest strikeouts per at-bat. And the very free-swinging nature that could be exasperating at times also contributed to Guillen becoming a very dangerous clutch hitter.

Of course, as the White Sox have discovered in his managerial abilities, it was Ozzie's intangibles that made him so valuable. As a player, he chattered even more than he does as a manager. Rickey Henderson was Guillen's favorite player to watch—and to distract with his constant chatter. Finally, New York had to call a team meeting, in which Willie Randolph stood up and admonished Henderson for letting Guillen get in his head.

That's not to say Ozzie was always the one causing the commotion. He's believed to be the one player in baseball history most victimized by the hidden-ball trick; he was nabbed by Greg Brock of the Milwaukee Brewers and Dave Bergman of the Detroit Tigers in 1989, and Boston

Red Sox second baseman (and former White Sox teammate) Steve Lyons in 1991.

Ozzie would play 1,743 games in 13 seasons with the White Sox and record 1,608 hits during that time. When his White Sox playing career ended in 1997 after the team bought out his $4 million 1998 salary, Guillen was decidedly introspective.

///If I hadn't prepared myself for this, I would be crying right now. This is not a broken heart, but I am unhappy. I am sad, but life still goes on. If this is the biggest problem a person is going to have, then shoot, he's a lucky person.[2] ///

Ozzie caught on with the Baltimore Orioles and would play three more seasons with Baltimore, the Atlanta Braves (appearing in the 1999 World Series), and the Tampa Bay Devil Rays, before retiring in 2000. He was a .264 career hitter, .273 in the postseason.

The end came for Guillen when the Devil Rays waived him before the start of the 2001 season. He was philosophical about the setback, and, as usual, retained his sense of humor.

///It's been great. I don't regret anything. Maybe my kids want me to keep playing, but it's time to move on. My country [Venezuela] has got three million people without a job—now they've got three million and one. ///

He was also confident that an end to his active career wouldn't mean an end to his life in baseball.

**❙❙** I can do whatever I want in baseball. I can pick my job. I can't say that I'm not [going to play], because you never know what's going to happen. But I don't want to go through this again. If some team calls me and wants me to play, I'd think about it twice. If they're going to use me for one year and then release me…I have to move all my stuff and meet all new people…it's worth it, but it's not. **❙❙**

As for whether he would be able to take a call during the 2001 season to play for the Devil Rays or some other team, Guillen had no worries.

**❙❙** I want to play as long as I can help a team win games. But I'm not going to kiss anybody's [behind] to stay in the game.

[Tampa Bay] said if something happened they might call me. They told me to stay in shape. I told them it's no problem. I stay in shape because I want to look good with clothes on. I don't stay in shape for baseball. I can play baseball getting out of bed.[3] **❙❙**

---

## chapter 2

# The New Hire

---

O zzie Guillen was named the 37<sup>th</sup> manager in White Sox history on November 3, 2003. In the process he became the first Venezuelan manager in baseball history.

Guillen was a bit of a surprise candidate. However, he was already held in high regard by White Sox fans, and his profile had only been raised by being the third-base coach on the 2003 World Series champion Florida Marlins.

His interview with GM Kenny Williams was spicy from the start. Williams told Guillen that former Toronto Blue Jays manager Cito Gaston was the frontrunner for the job, which irritated Guillen, who felt that he might be wasting his time if Williams' mind was already made up.

But the argument that ensued actually sold Williams on Guillen, and the rest is White Sox history. He was charged with taking over an under-achieving, unemotional team. Williams predicted that Guillen would deliver a "jolt" to players, and boy, was he right.

**Guillen:** I am excited and thrilled to be returning to Chicago to manage the White Sox. I have always been a White Sox at heart, no matter where baseball has taken me, and this is the job I always wanted. I wore this uniform 13 years. My heart always was here.

**Williams:** [Ozzie] bleeds White Sox baseball and he is going to provide something here that we desperately need. A jolt, if you will.

**Guillen:** Twenty-three years in baseball have helped prepare me for this day. I can't thank Jack McKeon and the Florida Marlins enough for the opportunity to coach third base and be part of a very special World Series–winning season.[4]

It was always my goal, my dream. It would be tougher for me to manage another team besides the White Sox because I wouldn't know the fans. I wouldn't know the people in the front office, the organization. Coming to the White Sox, I knew everything. All my life I've known baseball, the White Sox. I grew up here. I breathed, ate, talked baseball here. Everything here is around baseball.

One thing that didn't seem to bother Guillen from the start was the idea that from here on, every single decision he made would be analyzed and scrutinized.

///If you're worried about people second-guessing you, you better go and find something else to do for a living. Baseball is the easiest sport to second-guess in. People are always doing that. But people always enjoy second-guessing me more because I talk so much [stuff].

The truth is, I don't even know what I'm going to do once I'm out on the field, so don't bother trying to figure it out. //

Guillen didn't waste much time in trying to shake things up with the White Sox. He even saw fit to attack his office desk.

// They had this huge [bleeping] desk in here. You know what? You got a big [bleeping] desk, they just put a lot of [bleep] on it. They come in here with all this paper. I tell them, get that [bleep] out of here. I don't need that. //

## chapter 3

# A Rocky Rookie Year

O zzie soon found some controversy—and revealed a bit of naïveté—in his new role as manager. He came under criticism during spring training in 2004 for telling his players to "go get drunk or something" to forget about a loss.

*// I don't care what people think, if they second-guess or misunderstand what I say. Yes, I said it. I didn't think it would make it back home. I was talking with my team, and that's the way I'm going to communicate with them. //*

It's safe to say that right away, the White Sox realized that with Ozzie in the manager's chair, things would be very different. First off, contrary to the trends governing baseball for the past four decades or so, Guillen expected his starting pitchers to actually *pitch.*

*// I talked to [pitching coach Don] Cooper, and I want these guys ready to throw nine innings right from the get-go. I don't expect that to happen all of the time, but that's*

what I want. We have a young pitching staff, and I'm
going to let them go as far as they can. We have
one month to go, and if they can't get ready in
one month, they better get another job.

I won't hurt my pitchers, and I'm going to protect them.
But I'm going to give the kids a chance for me
not to baby-sit them. **//**

Guillen also encountered what he might have considered a kindred spirit in Japanese baseball veteran, 35-year-old major league "rookie" reliever, Shingo Takatsu. Stunned by Takatsu's poise in a new country and league—as well as his tantalizing "Frisbee" pitch—Guillen took to the pitcher.

**//**He was consistently hitting his spots and throwing strikes.
His delivery is smooth and relaxed. I don't want to tell
everyone what he has because I want them to be surprised.
But he was changing speeds and had great location.[5] **//**

As for the language barrier between Takatsu, who did not speak English, and Guillen, the manager expressed no worries.

**//**I want Shingo to be a part of this team. When
you are Japanese, don't speak English, and come from
somewhere else, there's a chance you could feel
left out or not a part of what's going on.
But we communicate well. He's a funny guy. **//**

Guillen has always been self-deprecating about his "mastery" of English, which is a line of joking he used for two straight years with his Japanese players. But he shared another joke when discussing the battle between closers Billy Koch and Takatsu at the beginning of 2004, this time in the pages of Venezuela's *El Universal,* where Guillen wrote a weekly column.

// When the media asked me yesterday who was
finally going to be the team's closer, my answer
was that the closer will be the one who closes! Not even
Yogi Berra would have responded better.[6] //

As the season neared, Guillen didn't pull any punches about what he perceived as a lack of heart on the team he inherited.

// They lost last year because their play was poor, not
because of [former manager] Jerry Manuel. They had great
talent. They didn't need a manager last year with the talent
they had on the field. That's an excuse. They have to do
better than that. I told them the first day in the meetings, "The
talent Kenny Williams put on the field for you guys? You
should have won that thing...you want to win? Play better
and don't make the manager make any moves."

I don't care if I shocked them or not. I said, "How many
managers can win a game for their team?" If you want to
win, don't give me a chance to [bleep] it up. Go throw
a shutout, and I'll just sit here and look smart.
Don't give me a chance to [bleep] it up. //

Ozzie also lifted a shot across the bow, warning his players that there would be no acceptable excuse for losing. This concept would play a big role in how the team was eventually reshaped in 2005.

*//* If we lose, what excuse are they going to make now? [Jon] Garland can't pitch because Jerry won't let him pitch past the fourth inning? Well, now we're going to see. Now I have [Garland] going longer. Now he has no more excuses.

Jose [Valentin] was hitting second or seventh, playing center field or left field or shortstop. Well, now he's the shortstop and we'll see what he can do.

Frank [Thomas] was hitting third, this guy wants to hit fourth. Okay, here's where everybody's going to hit. Now, what are you guys going to do? *//*

Paul Konerko, one of the streakiest hitters in recent White Sox memory, knew something was different in the clubhouse when his own manager started taunting him for his spring-training hitting woes.

**Konerko:** He would just laugh and say, you're terrible. Get over it. With Ozzie, from day one, it has been great. It has been a party.

The confidence Guillen instills in his players was evident from the very first game of 2004.

**//** My players make a difference. They don't play good
because of Ozzie. They play good because they start
believing in themselves.[7] **//**

The season was hard, with season-ending injuries to Frank Thomas and Magglio Ordonez taking the longball-dependent White Sox out of the Central Division race before September.

Guillen also learned that while it might be nice to expect his pitchers to go deep into games and/or pitch efficiently, his crew in 2004 simply wasn't up to snuff.

Late in the year, one of the hidden biases against Latin managers reared its head. Many GMs secretly were licking their chops at the prospect of Guillen as a manager, one going so far as to say that he "hoped we'd play that team [Guillen manages] 100 times a year." The supposition was that a Latin manager was not as bright as a Caucasian one.

In September, Texas Rangers manager Buck Showalter smugly called Guillen's knowledge of baseball rules and protocol into question. Afterward, when it was known that the rookie manager was correct to question his Rangers counterpart, Ozzie let Showalter have it.

**//** I never say anything about other managers.
If I have any bad comments I'm going to make, I'll keep
them to myself. But Mr. Baseball, who didn't even
have a hit in Triple A, says things like that.

He might be jealous. I have more money, more houses, and
more cars. And I'm better looking.[8] **//**

Ozzie's first season as a major league manager was quite respectable, finishing 83–79 and nine games behind the Minnesota Twins in the Central. With a healthy Thomas and Ordonez, could Ozzie's charges have taken the division in his rookie year? Perhaps.

But Guillen and GM Kenny Williams headed into the off-season determined to shake the team up in 2005.

*I know one thing. When they hired me, they didn't hire me to build a team. They hired me to win. And if we don't win, it's Ozzie Guillen's fault. The players win games. Managers lose games. You don't think that's true? When you're losing, who gets fired?*

*If we don't play good, I'll be the first one to tell Jerry and Kenny to get another guy in here. I'm the number one White Sox fan—I'm not just the manager. I want the White Sox to win, with or without me. But I hope it will be with me.*

## chapter 4

# Homeland: Venezuela

Ozzie's homeland is never far from his mind. He writes a weekly sports column for the Venezuelan newspaper *El Universal*. He wears No. 13 in honor of the Venezuelans who preceded him in the majors, namely Dave Concepcion.

Guillen was particularly close to the grandfather of the major leagues' great Latin American infielders, Venezuelan shortstop Chico Carrasquel. In fact, Carrasquel and Aparicio both attended Guillen's first game as manager in 2004 and threw out first balls alongside him.

*//I told the White Sox that we had to do that. I needed people to see that it wasn't just me who had become the first manager from Venezuela. These two men, Chico and Luis, they were the reasons I was here now.*

*Chico was having a tough time that day, but he wouldn't let me help him out of his wheelchair. He was proud to be there with me.//*

Guillen is part of a long line of Venezuelans who have played for the White Sox, including not only Chico Carrasquel and Luis Aparicio, but also Wilson Alvarez, Carlos Martinez, Fred Manrique, Magglio Ordonez, and Freddy Garcia.

*// In Venezuela, many people have a soft spot for the White Sox. So many Venezuelans have passed through here. Venezuelans have always known one of my goals has been to put my country on the highest pedestal. Because of that, they're happy.*

*The Venezuelan people who know me don't feel proud because we're winning. They're proud because they go, "How can this crazy man be the leader of a team?" //*

Carrasquel was a hero to millions, not just in his native Venezuela, but in Chicago, where he made his major league debut in 1950 after being plucked from Branch Rickey and the Brooklyn Dodgers. He was the third Venezuelan ever to play in the majors, and the first Latin player to appear in an All-Star Game.

In May 2005 Carrasquel died of a heart attack, and Venezuelan President Hugo Chavez called for two days of national mourning. Guillen, emotional but almost always under control of those emotions, struggled to accept that Venezuela's pioneer was gone. Months after

From left to right: Luis Aparicio, Ozzie Guillen Chico Carrasquel, and Dave Concepcio at Ozzie's first game as manage

Carrasquel's death, Ozzie left a press conference early—a sure sign that something's wrong with him—during the American League Championship Series rather than answer questions about Carrasquel, telling reporters, "You're going to make me cry." A week later, as the World Series began and Guillen was fast becoming the most popular Venezuelan on the planet, the manager was able to assess Carrasquel's importance.

**//** It wasn't easy for Chico to come to the United States and play baseball. He opened a lot of doors for us. He is one of the biggest reasons people make a lot of money and come from outside of this country to play baseball.

As the first great Venezuelan shortstop, Chico helped put our country on the baseball map. I am honored and proud to have known him as a friend. He was such a great friend, person, and role model for young players.

The thing I feel bad about is that he never had the opportunity to see this. He never had the chance to enjoy [a World Series]. I know where he is right now [but] he wishes he was here at this particular moment. In the meanwhile, he wishes us to be the best we can be.

That's why I was kind of sensitive about it. I always think about how bad he wanted this for the city of Chicago, for himself, for a lot of people. He was truly a baseball fan.

When I was asked about it [last week], the first thing
that came to my mind was that he was so
disappointed that it might be the last year he might
get to see it. All of a sudden, a lot of people were
going to enjoy this instead of him. **//**

Not everyone was aware of it, but when Chico was healthy, Guillen and
his hero would sit in the manager's office before games and talk baseball.
Carrasquel was a mentor to Hall of Famer Aparicio, who replaced
Carrasquel with the White Sox in 1959, the last season the club had
made it to the World Series. But Carrasquel, who did Spanish broadcasts
for the White Sox during a portion of Guillen's playing career and
remained close to the team, was the younger shortstop's hero, too. In
Ozzie's manager's office hang two photos of Carrasquel.

**//** We both felt it would be so wonderful if the World Series
came back to Chicago. Chico wanted me to have success.
He wasn't selfish or jealous. He was happy with what
he had and how he was treated by the White Sox.
Sometimes you feel guilty about winning before
somebody else does, and that's how I feel about Chico.

In Venezuela, not everybody likes me. Not everybody
likes Luis or Davey Concepcion. But you won't find
anyone there who didn't love Chico. **//**

Guillen also took time to eulogize his hero in the pages of *El Universal*.

> // He will be in another lineup, above,
> next to the other legends of baseball that have
> gone away before him.[9] //

The White Sox had honored Carrasquel by putting his No. 17 on the wall near the team dugout, and Guillen believed that his spirit was with the team.

> // He'd better be looking down on us. I'm going to
> come to him and say, just put your hands on us
> and we'll see what happens. //

Aparicio, who was honored along with some of his 1959 White Sox teammates in throwing out the first ball at Game 1 of the 2005 World Series, is another case entirely. He's an extremely private man, and Guillen considers himself one of the few in the Hall of Famer's inner circle.

> // I'm the only guy close to Luis. Not too many people are
> close to him. He is a different kind of guy. A lot of people
> have respect for him, but a lot judge him the wrong way
> because he's not very outgoing. //

After the World Series win, celebrations broke out and fireworks were shot in the streets of Venezuela. Ozzie took a call from President Hugo Chavez, who congratulated Guillen and celebrated him as a national hero. The president is a huge baseball fan and once dreamed of playing major league baseball.

**Chavez:** I dare to say you are like the king of Venezuela. Your triumph is the triumph for all of Venezuela.

**Guillen:** I'm going to try to bring the World Series trophy so that my country may enjoy what the people of the United States enjoy.

**Chavez:** You are a true leader, friend. The whole nation is waiting for you.[10]

A few days later, Guillen indeed did bring the World Series trophy down to Venezuela, where he was met with parades, a tribute from his former team, the La Guaira Sharks, and a reception from President Chavez.

///In Chicago they're thanking me for a championship,
here they're thanking me for making them happy.
For that reason, I had to bring the
World Series trophy to Venezuela.///

White Sox owner Jerry Reinsdorf had been worried that the trophy could be damaged or stolen in Ozzie's care, but the manager waved him off.

///I assured him that if it gets passed around
by drunken ballplayers after winning, it
wouldn't be broken in Venezuela.///

Guillen's mouth has often landed him in trouble. He looks people directly in the eye as he talks, lending the impression that his words leap straight from his heart to his lips. With that, he has an innate sense of fairness and equality, and to hear Ozzie tell it, that's also derived from his Venezuelan blood.

*"* I come from a country where we don't believe in treating people differently. When you're a person, you're a person. It doesn't matter what color or religion or race or sexuality you are. We're just human beings.

Obviously in this country it's a little bit different than our culture. I grew up in a country that was completely opposite from here. I worry about respecting people, the integrity of people. *"*

---

## chapter 5

# Crosstown Comments

---

Year to year, in good times and bad, the most charged baseball games in the city of Chicago are the ones that pit the White Sox against their crosstown rival Cubs.

Guillen played only one official city series, when the White Sox took two of three versus the Cubs in 1997. As a manager, he's more than made up for his lack of participation as a player by tweaking the Wrigley Field tradition and the perception that the Cubs are the city's more beloved team.

He entered the 2005 games having steered his White Sox to a major league–best 29–12 record, and treated the Cubs series as just another step toward a division title.

*// We're not going to change, I don't care who we're playing. It's no different facing the Cubs than Texas or Baltimore. We have a tough month ahead and we're not going to change anything about our style just because we're playing the Cubs. It's a big series for us—not because it's the Cubs, but because we're playing good baseball—and when you're fighting for first place, every series should be big. //*

White Sox vs. Cubs, June 25, 2004

Before the series even started, Guillen incited some controversy with his comments about the city series and Wrigley Field in general, including how upset he was that the Cubs didn't reserve a parking spot for him in 2004.

/// I think it's great when the game starts, but besides that, I hate Wrigley Field. It's not the Cubs fans, players, or the organization. It's Wrigley Field.

It's great for the city and fans to play on both sides [of town], but it's a lot of stress. But hey, I get paid for that. That's my job. ///

To his Venezuelan readers in *El Universal*, Ozzie attempted to explain the rivalry.

/// And so that the Venezuelans understand what this series means, imagine a Caracas–Magallanes game, and multiply the emotion by three.[11] ///

In 2005, the White Sox won two of three games at Wrigley Field, and the Cubs did the same thing to the White Sox at U.S. Cellular Field.

Perhaps partly smarting from the 5–7 record he has facing the Cubs, Guillen took time from the many obligations of his 2005 postseason to chastise Cubs manager Dusty Baker, who said he would not root for the White Sox in the playoffs, for his lack of support.

**Baker:** I got no one to root for. I sure as heck ain't rooting for the White Sox or Cardinals. Maybe the Braves since they've won all those divisions but only one title. The Angels just won it against me, so forget them. Anyway, fishing season starts in November. That's my time.

**Guillen:** I don't like what he said. I thought we were friends. That's OK, we'll see who owns the town now.

Still, Guillen made his pitch to Cubs fans to root for his White Sox, a concept that was heresy to some.

▐▌ I know there's a rivalry between the White Sox and Cubs, but this is one city. It doesn't say "South Side" on our chests, it says "Chicago." I hope the Cubs don't take it wrong, but Cubs fans and Chicago fans should be rooting for us. Why not? A lot of people didn't think we'd make it this far. ▐▌

# 2005: Wire to Wire

A fter the team-shifting trade that sent slugger Carlos Lee to the Milwaukee Brewers for speedster Scott Podsednik and reliever Luis Vizcaino, Ozzie attempted to justify the unpopular deal in the kickoff to the season, January's SoxFest. It was a barely veiled criticism of Lee that officially ushered in the era of the "new" White Sox.

> *// We're changing the shape of this team into something that fans will be excited to watch. Trust me, you're going to be proud of these guys [in 2005]. Last year, we had a guy slide into second base as if his wife was turning the double play. //*

Chicago's other slugging outfielder, free agent Magglio Ordonez, was another controversial offseason figure. The All-Star outfielder, recovering from a serious knee injury, had perceived that Guillen had been interfering with his contract talks. During the 2004 season, Ordonez had rejected the most lucrative contract ever offered to a White Sox player, one that would have paid him $14 to $15 million per season...before the injury.

After his injury, Ordonez vented his frustration against the White Sox, claiming that, among other things, the team lied to and betrayed him. He would eventually sign a lucrative, multiyear contract with the Central Division rival Detroit Tigers.

For Guillen, this betrayal by a countryman was beyond comprehension. His most colorful rant of 2005 would be his early-season tirade against Ordonez.

> **//** Magglio is another Venezuelan piece of
> [bleep]. [Bleep] him! He thinks I'm his enemy.
> Oh, I'm a big one now. He knows that
> I can [bleep] him over in a lot of different
> ways. He better shut the [bleep] up and
> just play for the Detroit Tigers.[12] **//**

Later, in his *El Universal* column, a calmer Guillen tried his best to clear the air.

> **//** I hope that [Magglio] is dedicated to playing ball,
> to enjoying his money, and that, when possible, he has
> me at the edge of his declarations. If he thinks
> I'm his enemy, that's his problem. **//**

Perhaps citing the underachieving nature of recent White Sox clubs, Chicago was tabbed to fall short once again in 2005. Most picked the White Sox for second place behind the Minnesota Twins, but some sources placed Chicago as far down as fourth place.

Such predictions raised the ire of a defensive White Sox club. GM Kenny Williams and Guillen, in particular, having deliberately reshaped the team to compete harder in 2005, scoffed at the cynicism.

The White Sox broke out of the gate, winning seven of 10, securing first place and never relinquishing it.

Observers immediately sought to name the White Sox's new style of play, reminiscent of the club's last World Series team, the 1959 "Go-Go" White Sox: Smartball, Smallball, Ozzieball, Grinderball.

*// Los gringos call this small ball, but in my dictionary I call it smart ball. I insist, if we continue playing like this and luck helps us out, we're going to give a little surprise to all of the analysts who've predicted third place for the White Sox in the Central Division. We'll see.[13] //*

Bright spots abounded in the early going. The team was pitching to the tune of a 3.28 ERA. None of the five starters had missed a turn. Although middle-of-the-order sluggers Jermaine Dye and Paul Konerko were both flirting with the Mendoza Line of .200, the White Sox had set a major league record to open the season for games in which they held a lead.

By the end of May, the White Sox stood 35–17, five games up in the Central Division. Guillen was rewarded with a contract extension through 2008.

**Guillen:** I will be the same guy. Nothing will change. I'll work harder than in the past because this is the team I'm going to manage for a few years—or as long as they want me to. This means I'll continue to do the best I can every day to make my team a winner.

**Williams:** He told me what he wanted. I gave him a little more than he wanted, and we had a deal. It took about 10 minutes. Now let's move forward and keep winning.

**Guillen:** I'm a fair guy. I'm not greedy. I get what I deserve. I'm happy with what I've done money-wise in baseball. A lot of people say, "If you were playing today or managing in this place or that place, you know how much money you could make?" I don't care. I've made a lot of money. People who wring their hands about the money they could have made here or there, that's no way to live. Maybe you were just born at the wrong time.

**Williams:** What's fair is fair. Ozzie has done everything we've asked of him from the time he was hired. He's done exactly what he said he'd do when we first sat down to talk about the manager's job, so this was a no-brainer. This is exactly the guy that we think it's going to take to get us to the next level.

He's got the exact attitude I want. He has the desire and passion for the organization and the city. His players know that, and I think he gets the most out of them.

Interestingly, in the White Sox's wire-to-wire division title, the team they punished the most over the course of the season was the division runner-up Cleveland Indians, winning 14 of their 19 games. And it was after a June 4 win against the Indians when Guillen revealed how much he relies on his battery to determine pitch selection.

/// I don't get involved in pitch selection. First of all, I am not that that smart. Second, I'm not that good. I trust my catchers. ///

Actually, Guillen, who is a follower of the Santeria religion, apparently is more willing to practice as a witch than count pitches.

/// It's true that [the White Sox have] been lucky, but the ingredients are there, on the field and on the bench, and even in the stands with the support of the fans. As for the rest, we have to keep it all together until October. From then on, it will be my turn to make witchcraft![14] ///

As the season wore on and the wins piled up, Ozzie was gaining confidence as a manager. It's not that he ever believed he could be anything but a great manager, but confidence and performance are two different things.

/// Last year I wasn't really managing. I was just making pitching changes. I feel like I'm a better manager, a manager who can do more things on the field, this year. Some of it is the new players I have. Some of it is knowing that I am a good enough manager to win in this league. ///

With the increased attention his winning baseball club was getting, Guillen also found that the spotlight was making him a little bit itchy.

**//** No sport lends itself more to criticism than baseball...who plays each position, where he bats in the order, what pitch you're going to request, what play you're going to make. Should the team play shallow or deep? And the outfielders? Do you bunt or hit and run? Do you give the pitcher one more batter, or do you bring in the lefty who's warming up? Devils! So many options. And the worst thing is that, whatever you do, there's always going to be someone criticizing your decision, even when the play goes well and you win the game. That's how baseball is.[15] **//**

Ozzie wasn't going to question the fast start of the team, but he was certainly aware that fortunes could turn.

**//** I love watching this team. The fans should be here to watch the kids play hard. Don't wait until September because we don't know if we'll still be there. Come enjoy what it is now. **//**

By June 8, "what it is" had become something very, very good. When the White Sox completed a road sweep at the Colorado Rockies with a resounding 15–5 win, the team sat comfortably atop the Central Division with a 40–19 record. The manager summed up what might be his shorthand managing philosophy.

/// I like my players to have fun, and when you're
winning, it's very easy to have fun. Getting clutch hits is more
important than anything else. That's what we've been
doing. Every day it has been somebody different.
We're not waiting for one hitter to be the guy. ///

While the *Chicago Tribune* focused some premature attention on the
White Sox's playoff chances, publishing a "magic number" countdown
beginning when the number was in the 50s, with plenty of season left to
play, Guillen preached caution.

/// I don't believe in a 10-game lead or an 11-game lead.
I believe in winning, and it's up to me to push these guys. ///

Of course, while the White Sox led the Central Division from wire to
wire, it can't be said that they didn't look back. From August 1, when the
White Sox had a 15-game division lead, to September 27, the team was
30–28. Respectable enough, but the trailing Indians went on a 37–14
tear in the same stretch, narrowing the White Sox's lead to as little as
one and a half games at one point.

On one hand, Ozzie objected to media calls of a "choke" by his team,
or that his 90-plus–win team could be characterized as a disappoint-
ment. On the other hand, the skipper knew that his team was playing a
little tight and getting away from what had made it so successful for the
first four months of the season.

/// We flat-out stink. Base running, bad pitching…if we
named what I'm disappointed about, we would be here all

week. Even the game we won, I was disappointed.
We came here and played real ugly baseball.
[After a 7–5 loss in Kansas City on September 15]

The people in Chicago know what's going on.
Are they stupid? No. What am I going to say after
we lose like that? My team is the greatest team ever?
I never regret anything I say. A lot of people think
I'm crazy or stupid. I'm ignorant. But come on…
we score nine runs against Kansas City and we still lose?
Do you think the people in Chicago want to hear me
say how great we are after that? The Chicago people
are way, way, way too smart for that.
[Before a 7–5 loss to Cleveland on September 19]

I'm not choking. We're not choking. If we lose, we lose. If I
win 96 games and you say 96 can win the division, I can go
home and relax. Chokers or losers, that's up to the fans. I
can only say that after the season is over, regardless of what
happens, I have great faith. I know we're going to win this
thing. I can walk everywhere with my head up.

I told my guys that we can't lose the division because I have
30,000 managers in the stands with me.

Right now, the only thing I have is faith. It's not over until it's
over. [Before a 7–6 win against Cleveland the next day]

I don't want to talk about how I feel about my team because I might say something you guys or my team don't want to hear. [After a 4–1 loss to Minnesota on September 22] **//**

Early in the 2005 season, Ozzie gave out his email address (ozzieguillen12@hotmail.com)…not to you or me, but to the *Sports Illustrated* readership, as well as to the readers of his weekly *El Universal* articles. As things were getting hairy in September, Ozzie would sometimes return to his office and throw up, and other times would need to sit down and have a cold pop, still shaking from the tension of the games, before addressing the media. Ozzie also issued reports on the state of his email inbox during his daily press conferences.

**//** I'm getting hundreds every day. Sure, I read them. I only like reading the nasty ones. It hurts me very much to read some of the comments, but I think there's something to learn from even the ugly criticism. More so than the ones patting me on the [back]. Of course, right now, there aren't many nice ones to weed out.

I'm interested in what people have to say when we lose. Sometimes it's funny, sometimes it makes me so angry I want to call or write to explain why I did what I did. I try to learn from it. Even when you do something right, if someone has another view of it, I can think for a minute and realize, wow, that guy's right. It helps me to always try to look at things from different angles. **//**

In the last week of the season, the Indians finally cooled off and the White Sox heated back up. Still, Ozzie seemed no less relaxed than always. He certainly wasn't counting magic numbers or such.

■■ I don't get involved with magic numbers and all that. I wasn't good in math. Just win today. That's the way I look at it. ■■

As the White Sox graduated from early-season surprise to legitimate World Series threat, the demands on ever media-friendly Guillen skyrocketed. But he was never fazed—and he knew how to keep even the most disappointing events on the field in perspective.

■■ I never feel tired from anything. You rest when you die, and then you'll be resting for good. When you're alive you should enjoy yourself and be the best you can be. You have to take advantage of being alive 100 percent because you don't know how much longer you'll be here.

After the worst storm and the worst hurricanes, the sun always comes out. This is true. It's also true that many thought that the unity that reigns in our clubhouse, the feeling that we're a family and all that happy atmosphere that they've envied us so much for, would collapse as soon as we fell into a losing streak. It was not like that.[16] ■■

## chapter 7

# The Importance
# of Family

On a team that features son Ozzie Jr. as an interpreter, as well as sons Oney and Ozney, it should come as no surprise that family is the most important thing in Ozzie's life. Family is even more important than wins, in fact.

Closer Dustin Hermanson suffered a family illness late in the midst of the White Sox's 2005 postseason run that jeopardized his availability at a time when the team was desperate for a consistent closer. Without hesitation Guillen cleared Hermanson to leave.

*// To me, family is more important than baseball. Baseball does a lot of stuff for us, but one day baseball will go away and family will be there for us. //*

The skipper had said the same thing when reserve infielder Willie Harris had to take bereavement leave in early May.

*// [Willie] wanted to stay and play this game, but family is more important. Baseball will kick your butt out of here. They*

don't care about you when you leave. Your family
will be there, and it's important that my players think
about family more than baseball. ///

As for Ozzie's own family, well, it bears repeating—there's nothing more important to him. He's said that if there's one goal he has—and this is before winning a division, pennant, or World Series as a manager—it's to see his grandchildren grow up.

/// My kids are the most important thing in the world to me.
I'm very close with my sons. I always keep them close. They
all have beepers or cell phones, and when I beep them, they
have 10 minutes to get home or one minute to call me.

A lot of things are worse than failure—killing somebody,
beating a kid. I just lose games. There are a lot of worse
things in life than losing a game. There are so many
terrible things in this world. I say, "Wow, God,
how much longer will you be so good, so nice to me? I get
up every day and say thank God I am who I am.
Thank God I have this life and the family I have. ///

---

## chapter 8

# A Division
# Series Sweep

---

Che White Sox finished in first place by six games after ending the season on a five-game winning streak—including a sweep of the year's final series, at Cleveland. By virtue of having the best record in the American League and the A.L.'s win in the 2005 All-Star Game, the White Sox were guaranteed home-field advantage throughout the postseason.

Their opening draw? The defending champion Boston Red Sox, in the same wild-card position as they used to streak to a World Series title in 2004. So the team whose title drought stood at 88 years, the White Sox, would have to defeat a Red Sox club that had just extinguished its own 86-year drought.

Guillen found himself struck by the massive obligations—none having to do with managing a baseball team—that the playoffs demanded. In the glint of an eye, the playoff roster needed to be set, charter flights and hotel accommodations finalized, pep rallies attended…

// Sometimes you just scratch your head like, "Why am I in this position right now?" It's fun to be in the playoffs, but it's a

lot of headaches. There are so many political things.
It drives you a little crazy. You have to do this and that.
I have to go to the pep rally and talk to our fans. What for?
They're going to show up and scream and cheer—they
don't need any pep talks from me. I just want to
make out the lineup and play the game. //

Contrary to his image inside the ballpark of being a wild and crazy guy, Ozzie doesn't seek the spotlight outside of it.

// When I'm not on the field, I want to be left alone. When
they pay you, they act like they own you. Even autograph
shows and those things, if you pay me, then you can
boss me around and tell me what to do. I'd rather do
it for free, leave when I want to, and give the money
to some charity. I don't want to be used. //

Not unexpectedly given the lack of respect accorded Chicago all season long, the White Sox were underdogs to win even a single playoff series. In fact, the White Sox were listed in Las Vegas as 10–1 favorites to win the World Series—placing them seventh of eight playoff teams, more favored only above the barely .500 San Diego Padres. But Guillen wouldn't dispute the White Sox's status as underdogs in the series.

// We know that we're underdogs. We've been underdogs
since April 1. Besides, who won the [2004] World
Series? They're the best team in baseball
until somebody else gets the flag. //

At the same time, Ozzie was fatigued by all the not-so-veiled disrespect of his team. He saw the White Sox as being too easily overlooked.

> // The way some people talk, it's like we played our games in Triple-A or something. Ninety-nine wins should get a little respect. It kills me that the Central Division is so overlooked. The best pitching staffs in the American League are in our division. Just because they don't make $100 million doesn't mean they're not good.
>
> But being overlooked isn't so bad. We kind of like it that way. //

After Chicago throttled the Red Sox 14–2 in Game 1, all the experts who figured that Boston would cruise past the less-experienced White Sox were nervously clearing their throats. Jose Contreras threw 7⅔ innings for the win.

> // Our pitching staff carried this team all the way to right now, and I still believe they're carrying us. //

Ozzie betrayed his usually calm dugout demeanor in the fourth inning, with his White Sox leading 6–1. The club had committed two consecutive fielding blunders, and the Red Sox were smelling blood in the water. With a runner on second and nobody out, third baseman Bill Mueller grounded to Tadahito Iguchi at second. Iguchi, rather than taking the safe, traditional out at first, instead threw across the infield to Joe Crede at third for the tag play. Runner Kevin Millar was out by miles, and the momentum shifted back to Chicago.

///I was saying, "No, no, no!" and then,
"That a boy, good job!" ///

Iguchi was the hero of Game 2 when he rallied the White Sox back from a 4–0 deficit to win 5–4 on a three-run homer in the fifth inning.

A twist in the game that allowed for Iguchi's heroics came with one out in the fifth. Juan Uribe hit a slow roller to second that looked like a sure double play, but Boston second baseman Tony Graffanino, a former White Sox, let the ball go through his legs. Guillen, an infielder whose rare miscues sometimes had similarly dire consequences, sympathized.

///If people think that was an easy play to make,
they're wrong. I have been there before, and
I know how it feels. It was not an easy play for him.
There was a lot of spin on the ball. ///

Boston catcher Jason Varitek led off Boston's sixth, looking to reverse the course of the game and knot the series at one. Once again, Guillen leapt into action, only this time not to react but to anticipate. Ozzie jumped to the top step of the dugout and wildly motioned for left fielder Scott Podsednik to play deeper. With the count 1–0, Varitek lined a shot down the left-field line, and it took a great jump by the fleet-footed Podsednik to track the ball down and steal at least a double.

*// I thought Podsednik was playing too close, especially the way the wind was blowing. Who knows? Maybe if I don't move him back he would have [still] caught it. But I don't like to do that—when you move a guy over, everybody in the ballpark sees you and the ball goes right to where the fielder was standing in the first place. Then you look like an [idiot]. //*

Coming in to save the game with a rare two-inning save was 6'3", 270-pound Bobby Jenks, who was pitching in Double A in July and was just one year removed from Class A Rancho Cucamonga.

*// I don't care how early in the game it was. I wanted to go with my best man, and he's my best man. //*

By the playoffs, Ozzie's email had evened out a bit. Aside from some Red Sox fans writing in to tell him to enjoy the playoffs while they lasted, Guillen was getting some positive feedback for his work on the season. One truly stood out.

*// It said, "Just go under the radar, keep saying what you're saying, that the White Sox aren't the favorites and you don't need to be. Just stay under the radar and keep winning. //*

Game 3 of the ALDS will be forever known for one inning, the sixth. Leading 4–3, reliever Damaso Marte loaded the bases on two walks and a single. With nobody out, Guillen turned to veteran hurler Orlando "El

Duque" Hernandez—a controversial pick over young ace Brandon McCarthy to make the playoff roster in the first place—to put out the fire.

Ozzie, for his part, had been all over home plate umpire Mark Wegner, contesting how starter Freddy Garcia and his relievers were getting squeezed. But despite some gestures and colorful language, Guillen knew to stop short in his protests.

*// I have to be there for my players. I'm not going to get tossed. You lose the respect of your team when that happens. I need my players, and they need me. I think people around the country have a bet on how many times I get thrown out of the game. //*

In a masterful bout of pitching, El Duque retired two Boston hitters on pop-ups and struck out Johnny Damon with a 3–2 curveball to preserve the lead. Hernandez pitched two more scoreless innings before giving way to Jenks to wrap the series up.

*// I went to El Duque because he's the only guy with more experience. He's had a lot of success against the Red Sox. Maybe someone else would show up nervous or anxious. El Duque has experience in the playoffs. //*

It was the first postseason series win for the White Sox in 88 years, and the manager could hardly contain his pride after his entire team toasted him in the locker room afterwards.

**//** Every day it's somebody different on this team.
I'm so proud of the players because they just go there to bust
their tails for all the fans and everyone in Chicago.
They do a tremendous job and they never panic.
That's why we are where we are.

For the franchise, it's great. The people in Chicago should
feel proud of these players. They did everything—every
day—and never failed. It's time to feel good about the
White Sox again. We're making it happen.

People are talking about the White Sox again and we should
feel good about it. They have waited a long time for
this moment. The team is making it happen this year.
When you pitch good, play hard, and execute well,
you should win—and we did. **//**

Fans mobbed Midway Airport to greet the team upon its return to
Chicago, taking players off-guard but delighting all. Naturally, the most
excited traveler was Ozzie.

**//** This is awesome. It's an awesome feeling. It's something
you feel proud about. You appreciate the fans doing
this for you. We were delayed a couple of hours,
and they still were there, out in the cold. The players
loved it, and I enjoyed it. Hopefully, we'll make them
prouder and win all the way to the end. **//**

---

## chapter 9

# Jerry and Kenny

---

I f Ozzie Guillen and Kenny Williams are brothers separated by two and a half months, White Sox owner Jerry Reinsdorf is the proud, if unlikely, papa.

In the summer of 1982 the White Sox drafted Williams in the third round even though he was said to have first-round ability, so the chairman made the then-unorthodox move of flying to California to persuade the Stanford football player to forego that sport in order to play with the White Sox. Two years earlier, Reinsdorf had found himself so excited to complete a trade for the 20-year-old Guillen that he called San Diego Padres owner Ballard Smith in the middle of the night to consummate the deal.

Williams and Guillen would play little more than two full seasons on the White Sox together, but they formed a friendship that is approaching its 20th year.

Both players have spent only scant years of their careers away from the White Sox. Guillen spent seven away as a player and coach; Williams three, after being traded from the White Sox in 1989 and retiring three years later.

Kenny Williams and Ozzie during 2005 spring training

Williams spent much of the 1990s working various jobs in the White Sox administration—in marketing, negotiating broadcast deals, and heading up minor league operations—before ascending to the GM chair at the end of the 2000 season.

**Guillen:** A lot of managers tell their GM what they want to hear. I won't do that. I won't lie to him. I won't talk to him as a boss. I'll fight him.

**Williams:** I sit at the head of the table, so I'm always able to get a word in when Ozzie's on one of his runs. He respects me as GM, but not too much. He loves to tell me when I'm wrong. What's important is that sometimes I defer to him, and sometimes he defers to me.

**Catcher Chris Widger:** We have a checks-and-balances system. Ozzie says whatever he wants, and Kenny is the voice of reason. But no manager and general manager have more of a passion to play the game the right way and win.

**Williams:** I would watch Ozzie on the bench try to persuade [former White Sox manager] Jim Fregosi to change pitchers or call a pitchout. Right then, it seemed to me that Ozzie had the desire and ability to manage.

**Hitting coach Greg Walker:** I played with both guys and they seemed like total opposites. But they got to be close friends.

Three years after being named general manager, Williams made Guillen his first managerial hire. The GM–manager relationship started off with some fire and hasn't much cooled since.

**Williams:** Cito Gaston and I had talked, and I was comfortable with him as my choice as the new White Sox manager. So when Ozzie arrived, I was blunt with him. I told him he really had some convincing to do if I was going to make him our manager. It was the start of, shall we say, a very lively conversation.

**Guillen:** I don't know exactly that I yelled at him, but he made me feel as if I was wasting my time coming up [to Chicago] and talking with him. I said to him that if you think I can't do this job, just tell me right now.

**Williams:** It was lively, a fun talk. The most enjoyable interview I've had. But I felt I had to ask him why he came all the way up from Miami to interview if he was going to quit so easily.

But his fire, his passion for a job he was a long shot to get showed me something right there. If we didn't value the same things, pitching and defense, I wouldn't be standing here talking to you about Ozzie Guillen as my manager. But Ozzie's fight, the passion he was clearly going to bring to the job, that became his best selling point. And I bought it.

This team needed some toughness, someone with pride, and someone who truly loved our organization. And you can't find a better candidate under those criteria than Ozzie.

Williams also is well aware that a big part of the Ozzie package are the two lips that go flippity-flop. But the GM claims that there's little that Ozzie blurts out that ever really disturbs him.

Ozzie with Jerry Reinsdorf, right, and Illinois Speaker of the House Michael Madigan at the State Capitol on November 2, 2005

**Williams:** I've anticipated most of what Ozzie's said, believe it or not. So sometimes I know what the reaction will be before he even says it. He usually makes me laugh. Sometimes, I wonder what he's thinking, and say to myself, "I'm glad he said that and not me." A few times, he's upset me.

If the most troublesome thing about Ozzie is his honesty, is that really such a big problem? We're very guarded today. So Ozzie soils the sanitary nature of sports today. Is a little bit of color or flavor such a bad thing?

**Guillen:** To me, honesty is like you are planted firmly on the ground. Nothing can sway you. But when you're honest, you can hurt people. But at least you're honest and tell the truth. Not too many people are like me. Most people put themselves behind a wall, but deep inside they want to say what I do. They just don't have the guts.

By the end of 2005, Williams was the only African American GM in baseball, and Guillen was one of only two Latin managers.

**Reinsdorf:** I never put two and two together before Kenny hired Ozzie, but they do behave an awful lot like brothers. They fight and disagree like two brothers. But they are of one mind when it comes to winning baseball, and for us, that's the most important quality for them to share.

The admiration that both Guillen and Williams have for their boss is remarkable. There is an intimacy among the three that is uncommon in any sport.

*II* Jerry is the greatest man I've ever met. I don't say that because he signs my paycheck. I say it because he's a straight man who won't lie to you. He gets treated very badly in [Chicago]. It's not fair to him. Jerry means well for everybody. He should be more respected for that. I hope one day he will be. *II*

# The White Sox
# Win the Pennant!

There was much hand-wringing over the next White Sox oppo-
nent, the Los Angeles Angels of Anaheim, who had historically
been very successful against the White Sox. On the West Coast,
the White Sox had mustered a mere 15–39 record at Anaheim in the
prior decade, and 5–15 since the 2001 season. But if there was any worry
over playing this foe, it wasn't coming from the manager.

> // To me, it's a new ballgame. The problems that we have
> had in the past on the West Coast, most of the time
> we started in Oakland, where the pitchers gave us
> problems. Then we would move on to Anaheim
> in a slump. I'll take my chances now. //

The White Sox opened the 2005 American League Championship Series
at home, facing a severely jet-lagged Angels team that had just defeated
the New York Yankees the day before. Still, most experts saw similarities
between the two clubs and granted the edge to the Angels.

Despite being the underdog, the White Sox, with three days off after the Boston series, were expected to pounce on the tired Angels and cruise to a Game 1 win. As often happens, the reverse came true.

Paul Byrd shut down the White Sox, 3–2, and the White Sox wasted another strong start by Jose Contreras, who surrendered only two runs in eight and a third innings. Chicago appeared flat and in danger of another patented White Sox postseason offensive shutdown. Guillen appeared to agree.

> ⫻ We failed today at moving the guys over. We don't have the type of team that's going to score 20 runs. ⫻

The White Sox played much of Game 2 as if they'd be lucky to score 20 runs in an entire seven-game series, scoring one run on six hits through eight innings. The bats had been put in deep freeze by Anaheim pitching, and Chicago was one flick of the bat away from an 0–2 hole in the series.

Then, with two outs in the bottom of the ninth in a 1–1 game, catcher A. J. Pierzynski executed the ultimate hustle play—sprinting out a third strike that appeared to have hit the ground—and one batter later, the series was deadlocked. Guillen, a grinder as a player and a manager, applauded Pierzynski's heads-up play.

> ⫻ If we win the series, that play will be around forever. If we lose, everybody will forget about it. The umpires are human, not robots. If you look at the replay, it was not an easy call to make. Put yourself in that situation, it was so close and so quick.

Ozzie and fellow Venezuelan Freddy Garcia in the dugout during a 5–4 Sox win over the Angels on May 30, 2005

> This is a game about inches, and we took advantage
> of the two inches that helped us today. I always say
> I'd rather be lucky than be good, and the ball
> bounces this way and we take advantage of that.
> Two teams play the game. One team gets a break and
> takes advantage, it means the other team allowed it to
> happen. So don't forget what we did to win the game. //

Game 3 in Anaheim wasn't sullied by controversy of any sort, as Jon Garland, who hadn't pitched in 13 days, shut the Angels down and steered the White Sox to a 5–2 win. Garland was helped by a two-run homer in the first inning by Paul Konerko, the eventual series MVP.

**Guillen:** We didn't know which Garland would show up because he's been off for so many days. I was concerned, but not worried. But when we scored in the first inning, the dugout started getting happy. Every time we score first early, we seem like we play better baseball. The first inning set the tone.

**Garland:** Ozzie's definitely shown faith in me. He's let me find out a lot about myself by giving me a chance to succeed. It's fun playing for him because he's like another player—a crazy one—on the team with us, who keeps everyone loose and makes everybody laugh.

White Sox starters had thrown all but two outs of the series so far, and had completely shut down Angels slugger Vladimir Guerrero, who would finish 1-of-20 for the series. Guillen, whose first coaching job was with the Montreal Expos—Guerrero's former team as well—knew the superstar too well to comment on his slump.

*// I don't want to say anything bad about Vlad because I don't want to wake him up. Our pitching staff is doing a tremendous job all year long against him. //*

Ozzie's friendly relationship with Guerrero also was a flashpoint for criticism. While Guillen pal and third-base coach Joey Cora wouldn't even speak to his own *brother,* a Red Sox infielder, during the ALDS, Guillen hugged managers, players, announcers, vendors...anyone from the opposition.

*// People say that I don't have respect for the game because I'm talking to people I'm not supposed to. Believe me, I'm hugging Vlad right now, but if we had to hit him [with a pitch], he's the first guy I'll pick. That's the way I am.*

*Vlad Guerrero was my friend before I was a manager, and he's going to be my friend when I leave managing. //*

Suddenly ahead in the series, Guillen took time to assess again where he would land after the season, after stating previously that he might quit if the White Sox won the World Series. Now, he provided one possible destination.

*// If we win the World Series, I might be the next mayor of Chicago. //*

Game 4 was another pitching gem by the White Sox, with Freddy Garcia going the distance in the 8–2 win to make it three straight complete games for Chicago. On this stellar pitching staff, in the words of White Sox pitching coach Don Cooper, "they all want to be the lead dog." Ozzie agreed.

// Freddy wants to follow his teammates, what they did a couple of days before, and he wanted to be part of that, too. It's nice when you have four guys you can count on. //

It was an on-and-off drizzle, of all things, that marked Sunday, October 16's ALCS Game 5—the first chance in almost five decades that the White Sox would have to clinch a World Series berth. They would not be denied, winning 6–3. Nor would the starting pitchers be denied; the only starter not to throw a complete game yet in the series, Contreras, used his second start to right that wrong. It had been 50 years since a team's starters had completed four consecutive games in the postseason.

// The biggest reason we are where we are is because of Jose. Every time we need a big game, he got it for us. //

Having delivered the White Sox their first pennant in 88 years, Guillen still opined that the team accomplished the feat as much in spite of him as because of him.

// We took a lot of beatings during the season and just kept on playing. Good thing my players don't listen to what I was saying to the media. We stuck together. //

---

e Contreras is removed by Ozzie with one out in the ninth inning of Game 1 of the )5 ALCS. It would be the only call to the bullpen Guillen would make all series.

## chapter 11

# Inside the Clubhouse

They're all his "kids." Ozzie refers to every player on his roster—even a player as old as Frank Thomas, all of four years his junior—as "kids."

It's easy to assume that Ozzie gets along with his kids—er, his players—so well because he's still close to playing age, and he generally acts like he's just a worn-in glove away from stepping back on the field himself.

But that behavior can work two ways. Become too much of a big brother or buddy to your team, and a manager can be taken advantage of, unable to enforce any rules or discipline.

Contrary to his public perception as a constant jokester, Ozzie knows that working closely with him can come at a cost.

> /// I can get mad really quickly. So quick that sometimes nobody knows about it. Everyone thinks I'm always having fun and making jokes, but I can get mad really quick. The good thing is that I get over it really fast, too. I'm like a match. ///

Guillen has managed to walk that fine line without even trying. It starts with his willingness to treat his players like adults, and trust that they will do the job they're paid to. His most important rule is: no excuses.

///I don't try to take heat away from my players because I throw my players under the bus a lot of times. I just pick the right time to do it. I lead the league in throwing my players under the bus.

I want my players to not point fingers or blame each other. The most important thing to me is to support a teammate, even when he's made a mistake. You have to believe in yourself, and play for each other.

When something happens, it always has to be somebody's fault. That's why I say if something happens in this ballclub, blame it on me. I will always blame myself before somebody else will. I'm not going to give people ammunition. I'm not going to give excuses. Yeah, blame it on me.

Me and the players are friends, but we have to respect each other. I respect you, you respect me, respect my rules, respect your teammates, respect the fans, respect baseball. That's all I'm going to ask of you.///

In spite of acting like a teenager much of the time, Guillen has a sense of decorum. He didn't rush into the team pileups that marked each

Ozzie and Frank Thomas

postseason series victory, instead embracing his sons and watching from the dugout, like a proud father.

Guillen also recognizes the importance of knowing when to shut his door to players.

> ▰▰ I hate it when a manager says that his door is always open. I'm not like that. My door is always closed. I keep that door closed for my coaches and my media people. You can talk with players on the field, in the dugout, on the bus, in the clubhouse, on the golf course, in the bar. Everywhere I turn I see players, so I have to shut the door sometimes. ▰▰

When his players don't work hard and respect the game, their alliance with the manager can sour quickly. Shortstop Juan Uribe was called into Guillen's office after a July loss at Oakland for not running out a fly ball, and any comfort zone Uribe thought he had with Ozzie evaporated in a snap.

> ▰▰ I'm going to show my players I'm here for real—not because we're friends, not because we get along well and I let the players do what they want to do. If they think that, they got the wrong man. If they feel comfortable, I'm not. If we think we're that good, we're not.
>
> I might lose for a reason—being a bad manager or a bad team. But I'm not going to lose because my team didn't give me its best effort. ▰▰

Actually, Guillen is a real stickler for one thing: the national anthem. If anyone is late for the anthem, the fine is $500.

///That's the thing that pisses me off the most. Two reasons.
If you're not from this country, you should respect the anthem
even more than Americans because you should feel pleased
you're here. And if you're from this country, you
should have respect for people who are dying for it.
This is a great country. It has the right of free speech.
That's why a lot of countries have problems,
because [people] can't speak for themselves.[17] ///

In fact, for a man who has yet to be granted his U.S. citizenship, he is incredibly patriotic. In anticipating the playoffs in 2005, he revealed that his favorite moments of his previous postseason appearances came before the game even started.

///Every time they play the national anthem here
I look for the planes. I can't wait to see the planes fly over
our field in the World Series. That's the greatest feeling
anyone in baseball can ever feel, standing on the
baseline and seeing the planes fly over. It gives
me goose bumps just thinking about it. ///

You get the sense that Ozzie is going to be just as active an American citizen as he is in Venezuela, where his charities have raised the hopes of innumerable Venezuelans.

// We get united when something bad like the hurricane in New Orleans happens. But why can't we be like that every day? Why can't we be together every day, no matter what race, politics, and religion we are? //

At the 2005 trading deadline, there was much talk about what trades the White Sox should make in order to secure a division title, as if their league-best record didn't prove that the pieces were already in place. Ozzie felt a need to defend the guys who had brought the White Sox to the top of the baseball world.

// We're not going to bring a player here just because he's good. We'll bring a player here to play the way we play and believe on the field and off the field. We don't want a superstar just so people can be excited about getting that guy. I want a good player on the field and off the field.

I told Kenny not to fix something that's not broken. It's not fair to break up or disrupt my team after they've played so good for me. //

If there's any magic in Ozzie's methods—or even his madness—it's the unity that his trust had engendered. He looked back at 2005 and recognized how much of a team he had built.

// I have good ballplayers, though we didn't have the greatest talent on earth. We had the greatest team, though.

Nothing in this world is achieved with talent alone. It's done with unity. My greatest strength was having the confidence to know that any of my players could do the job. //

White Sox fans have had a love-hate relationship with third baseman Joe Crede over the years, but one man who has always stuck up for him is Guillen.

// I have a feeling that Joe Crede will be a tremendous ballplayer, and I see this kid every day. He's great defensively, he's a strong kid, he plays the game right. It's a matter of time before he has a breakout year. These guys who have potential, you have to be careful with them. //

Guillen proved to be correct. Crede battled injury and had, on paper, a decent 2005 season offensively. But he was one of the best clutch hitters on the team and had a Gold Glove–quality season in the field. And Crede had a brilliant postseason, during which he could have been named the MVP of the ALCS, World Series, or both. The fact that Crede has accomplished all he has with two herniated disks in his back has earned the everlasting respect of Guillen.

// This kid's a gamer. Only he knows how bad his back is. He told me as long as he can take the pain and go to the field, he will. If you watch him every day, he should be a Gold Glover. And at the plate he's capable of carrying the team for two or three weeks. He's that good. //

Right fielder Jermaine Dye had big shoes to fill in Chicago, taking over the spot where Magglio Ordonez had built his superstar résumé for eight years.

Dye famously held his word to the White Sox that he would sign with the team in the 2004 offseason even after receiving better subsequent offers. That strength of character meshed well with Ozzie's.

**Dye:** I think Ozzie's personality rubbed off on everybody. He's a laid-back guy. He'll say whatever is on his mind and he keeps everybody loose. He wants you to go out and have fun, stay positive, no matter if you're down. Ozzie just knows how to win.

For his part, Guillen stood by his new outfielder even when Dye took a below-.200 average deep into the season.

// There's more there, believe me. He's not going to be a .200 hitter all season. He's pretty close to swinging in the bat better. The one thing about Dye is that no matter what he does at the plate, he doesn't carry it into the field. //

Reliever Dustin Hermanson was another newcomer to the White Sox, and when incumbent closer Shingo Takatsu faltered, "Hermie" was the one who closed out games for the balance of the season, in spite of debilitating back pain that required extra care.

// He's a warrior, no matter where you put him. He'll give you everything he has. As long as this kid's healthy, he's going to do good. //

In the 2004 offseason, the White Sox signed Orlando Hernandez, not much of a blockbuster on paper but an astute move by Kenny Williams. The Cuban-born "El Duque" became an unofficial pitching coach most responsible for guiding younger Cuban star Jose Contreras to a brilliant second half and postseason. And El Duque proved he had some innings left in him, too—none bigger than a bases-loaded, no-outs sixth-inning relief appearance in Game 3 of the ALDS in Boston. Hernandez fell behind the first hitter he faced, Jason Varitek, 2–0, and went to three-ball counts on the next two, Tony Graffanino and Johnny Damon. All three were retired, the latter two after forcing El Duque to throw five pitches to them with full counts. Afterward, Hernandez praised his manager.

**Hernandez:** No one believes this, but the success we have had is a lot due to Ozzie. When he makes a move, none of us complain. I would have loved to be a starter in one of the games, but I didn't deserve it this time.

**Guillen:** This kid...I don't know if I should call him a kid...I knew he would bring cold blood.

Throughout the season, one of Guillen's favorite players was rookie second baseman Tadahito Iguchi, a veteran of the Japanese leagues who honed his coordination as a young man by playing badminton with his mother. Iguchi's focus, fundamental play, and all-around skill earned Ozzie's admiration. Guillen's first question to Iguchi in spring training was whether or not he spoke English. When Iguchi said no, Guillen said, laughing, "Neither do I."

//When he came to the U.S. he had to change
his game for us, and he did. Every time we need
to get something done, he has done it.
He has been overshadowed by a lot of people.

If Iguchi was hitting sixth, seventh, or fifth, I bet he'd hit
.300 and 20-something home runs. I take a lot of at-bats
away from him. One of the big reasons we are here is
Iguchi. The kid does everything for the team, and
that's why I keep saying this kid is my MVP.//

Indeed, after the season, Guillen announced that Iguchi would move down in the lineup so that the White Sox could take advantage of his power.

Paul Konerko proved to be the cornerstone of the 2005 World Series champions. In fact, when Konerko re-signed with the White Sox in the 2005 offseason, Guillen named him team captain.

//Paulie does everything in his power for us to be what we
are, on the field and off. This kid is my leader.//

But the first baseman is quick to acknowledge just how well equipped Guillen is as a manager.

**Konerko:** The coaching staff is well-prepared for any situation. I know Ozzie has a reputation for all the crazy stuff, but our guys are organized. They have always been students of the game, and they're always studying while it's going on.

Damaso Marte was the one cautionary tale of the 2005 season that told players what *not* to do under Ozzie. Despite the fact that Guillen had been more than patient with the inconsistent young left-hander, Marte started flouting team rules late in the season and found himself suspended from the team and ostracized immediately.

*// I have a rule on my team. If you're not on the disabled list and late, you're not going to be on my team. Is he a distraction? For me, yeah. For the team, no. We can play without him. We've done it before. //*

In spite of growing fan angst and a limited number of pitchers allowed to play in the postseason, Guillen stuck with Marte after he apologized to the team, keeping him on the White Sox roster until the last out of the World Series. Still, the enigmatic lefty continued to walk batters and lose focus in the postseason, a big no-no in the manager's bible.

*// He put the team on the line. I don't mind if you get beat, but don't beat yourself. If you get beat, that's fine. Hey, everybody goes out there and gets beaten. But when you go down there and don't want to throw the ball and you're flat with pitches, that shows me you don't have confidence in yourself. //*

Even at the height of his frustration with Marte, Guillen realized that he might have to use him in the very next game, so he had to invoke his own rules with how he treated the pitcher.

// Nobody trusts his bullpen more than Ozzie Guillen.
I have to give him that ball. That's trust. I have
to use him, whether people like it or not.
That's what I have to work with. //

Rookie pitcher Brandon McCarthy had an enigmatic start to the 2005 season, with a few solid outings sprinkled among inconsistent starts, carrying an eight-plus ERA. When Hernandez returned from the disabled list in July, the White Sox sent the 21-year-old back down to Triple A.

// I fell in love with this kid in spring training. I thought he
was going to throw the ball better, but he hasn't done it yet.
It's not fair to make him stay here and suffer the way
he does and make me suffer the way I am. //

By season's end, however, McCarthy had been recalled and was stellar in his last six starts. In fact, as the White Sox wheezed down the stretch and the starting rotation was getting roughed up in September, there were some who called for McCarthy to enter a potential postseason as the team's number one starter. Guillen was having none of it.

// The kid's been here, what, 10, 20 days?
That's just stupid. //

At season's end, with the ship righted, the White Sox opted for experience over momentum and made the hard decision to leave McCarthy off of the playoff roster entirely.

Another one of Guillen's favorites is hardscrabble catcher A. J. Pierzynski, who joined the White Sox in 2005 saddled with a reputation for being a bad teammate. Ozzie found that Pierzynski's reputation couldn't have been more inaccurate.

*// A.J. is a 20-something-year-old baby. He says stuff, and people sometimes don't like it. I just laugh. The only thing about A.J. is he just wants to win. //*

No White Sox player commanded as much attention as Frank Thomas. Since Ozzie took over as manager, most of the attention paid to Thomas has been negative regarding his foot and ankle injuries or his dour attitude. Guillen, who wasn't close to Thomas when the two were White Sox teammates, didn't waste any time once he was hired as manager to address Thomas.

*// Frank was a great teammate, but I hear a lot of negative things about Frank. I'm sorry, but Frank will play my way. I hear negatives about Frank, but I want him to be how he was in the early 1990s when I was here. I love Frank. I need him here and I need him to be a great player in the clubhouse.[18] //*

In fact, Guillen felt his comments about the future Hall of Famer were too strong and apologized to the slugger the next day.

*// That was the worst day I ever had in my career, because that day I was hurting Frank Thomas's family and the White Sox organization. //*

Thomas would have a strong season in 2004, truncated by injury, and as he neared his return from rehab in 2005, Guillen shot a few more comments over the bow.

> *// It is good to have Frank here, because now he can see a winning attitude. He was a big part of the bad attitude [in 2004]. Now he can see the guys, how we handle stuff, why we're not whining every day. Everybody is happy, and I want Frank to be part of that. //*

While Thomas was slow to come back and had taken his share of shots from Guillen in the past couple of years, he had no worries over whether he could fit into the 2005 White Sox.

**Thomas:** As for Ozzie and I, we're cool. We've always been cool. We know each other like brothers, and Ozzie's not going to hold his lip for anybody. He's said things in the past and we've worked through them.

When it comes to offensive production, Ozzie is also unabashedly one of Thomas's biggest supporters. He's repeatedly named Thomas as the best hitter he's ever seen, and when Thomas burst back into action with a flurry of home runs in June 2005, Guillen was in awe.

> *// Frank is Frank. He is going to do what he can to win games for us. He is one of the best, if not the best, ever to wear the White Sox uniform. Anytime he comes to the plate, you think something is going to happen. //*

Thomas was reinjured after 34 games, but remained with the team to lend support in the postseason. It was there that Thomas could assess— perhaps better than anyone—the impact Ozzie had on the White Sox.

**Thomas:** Ozzie told us from day one how it was going to be, and I know a lot of people were wondering how we were going to fit in and all this other [stuff]. I know he wants to win. He made guys care about the team, and that's the biggest thing is making guys care. Nobody gave [the White Sox] a chance, but Ozzie made them believe.

If there's a player on the White Sox who should most remind Guillen of himself, it's shortstop Juan Uribe—and not so much for the shortstop part. In the field, both players are skilled—Guillen was graceful, Uribe is powerful.

The similarity comes at bat. Guillen never saw a pitch he didn't like, and the same can be said for Uribe. It's a guarantee that if Uribe actually watches a called strike, he's swinging at the next pitch, no matter where it is.

Recalling Uribe's game-changing triple off of New York Yankees überreliever Mariano Rivera in August, Guillen could have clipped the notes out of a scrapbook from his own career.

*// * It's crazy because Uribe can't hit a guy who throws junk, and all of a sudden he hits the best guy in the majors. *//*

---

## chapter 12

# A Historic
# World Series

---

O n the eve of the World Series, Guillen was named Manager of the Year by *The Sporting News*. Typically, he deflected credit and joked over the honor.

**//** The only thing I can say is that it's a nice trophy, but the players do it for you. Without these players, I'm not winning any trophies. In fact, winning one of these usually means you're going to get fired, so I guess it's been a nice run, see you later. **//**

The 2005 World Series began on October 22, 2005, with the Houston Astros arriving in Chicago to take on the White Sox. In spite of winning 10 more games during the regular season and compiling a 7–1 record so far in the playoffs, the White Sox were still only about an even-odds pick to win the World Series; most observers favored Houston's starting trio of Roger Clemens, Roy Oswalt, and Andy Pettitte over the White Sox hurlers, who had just thrown four straight complete games.

Most of the attention centered on Clemens in Game 1, but the Astros fireballer lasted only two labored innings before leaving. Guillen had no complaints.

*// Of course I was relieved. Roger is going to be a Hall of Famer. When you make this guy leave in the second inning, no matter who you bring in from the bullpen, he isn't going to be better than Roger. Our offense worked him real well to get him out of there. //*

The "Big Boy," White Sox reliever Bobby Jenks, stole Clemens's fire-balling thunder with a four-out save and an eighth-inning faceoff with Houston slugger Jeff Bagwell that saw Jenks toss five straight 100 mph–plus pitches in a row.

Guillen had adopted a comical signal to indicate when he wanted Jenks to come into the game rather than Dustin Hermanson: arms spread wide and high to indicate he was calling for the, er, "big and tall" pitcher. Ozzie nonchalantly defended the gesture.

*// I don't want to embarrass the kid, but I want the big boy. //*

Jenks took the slapstick call in stride.

**Jenks:** I think it's pretty funny calling the big guy in. I know Ozzie does a lot of things out of humor. He doesn't mean anything by it.

Ozzie waves to fans at University Stadium in Venezuela while his son Oswaldo, holds the World Series trophy on November 4, 200

Game 2 of the Series was an epic battle, with Houston rallying with two runs in the top of the ninth to even the game, 6–6, against the seemingly indefatigable Jenks. But just when the White Sox seemed vulnerable to deflation and letting a game in hand slip away, up stepped leadoff man Scott Podsednik with one out in the bottom of the ninth to face Brad Lidge, Houston's own unhittable closer. The five-year vet, who had hit zero homers during the regular season, launched a shot into the right-center stands and, just like that, the White Sox were up 2–0 in the World Series. Seeing Podsednik pick up Jenks with his big hit came as no surprise to Guillen.

*That's the way we play all year. We keep fighting, making a big pitch. When somebody falls, somebody else picks them up. This team has a lot of unity.*

Game 3 was the longest in World Series history, with the Astros well aware that a loss in their first game in Houston could seal their fate. With ace Roy Oswalt on the mound, there was reason for confidence.

After four strong innings and with a 4–0 lead, Oswalt lost his composure. The White Sox plated five runs and batted around in the inning. Oswalt also hit Joe Crede with a pitch, which incited a shouting match between dugouts (primarily Astros manager Phil Garner and White Sox outfielder Carl Everett).

*No, I don't think Oswalt was throwing at Joe. A lot of people were confused because Joe was talking to himself. I look on the other side of the dugout, and people are screaming to Joe. Joe never said anything to Oswalt.*

Nobody's happy when you get hit, but all of a sudden they were talking. Obviously my bench is going to be going crazy, too, when that happens. **//**

The White Sox edged ahead on utilityman Geoff Blum's fourteenth-inning home run. But Guillen later admitted that Blum almost didn't make it into the game.

**//**I had Pablo Ozuna in the double switch in the thirteenth, and all of a sudden I looked at my lineup and saw Blum, and he's a switch-hitter. He plays a little bit better at second than Pablo. So I switched my mind, and it worked out for us. **//**

The fourth game was yet another nail-biter. A 1–0 duel that was score-less through seven innings. The pivotal eighth inning began with Willie Harris pinch-hitting for starting pitcher Freddy Garcia. He singled off of closer Lidge and was sacrificed to second on a bunt by Podsednik. Carl Everett moved Harris to third on a ground out, which brought World Series MVP Jermaine Dye to the plate. Dye grounded a Lidge slider right up the middle for a single to bring in Harris, and the White Sox pushed ahead.

It was fitting, however, that defense—a White Sox strong suit all season long—was the watermark of the team's World Series clinch. Unheralded shortstop Juan Uribe sprinted deep into the stands to catch a foul pop for the second out of the ninth, and his slapdash sprint and throw on Orlando Palmeiro's dribbler up the middle clinched the Series.

**//** We built this team around defense
and pitching. When I saw Uribe make the
last play, I knew he was going to make it.
Our defense is one of the biggest reasons we
won the World Series, no doubt about it.

But at the end there, yeah, my heart
was pounding 2,000 mph. **//**

It may have been the closest sweep in World Series history, but it was nonetheless a sweep. The White Sox had completed an 11–1 playoff run and outscored their opponents in the postseason by more runs than any team in history.

In the process of winning it all, Ozzie became the first manager born outside of the United States to win a World Series. In spite of having more energy than even his youngest players, Guillen was restrained as his team celebrated on the field.

**//** I wanted to watch my team—my boys—celebrate
out there. A lot of people thought because the
way I am I was going to be jumping around with all
my players, but I was happy just to watch my boys,
jumping back and forth, all over the place. **//**

Soon, the questions were asked of Ozzie...how did he make an impact on this world champion baseball team?

Jerry Reinsdorf, Kenny Williams, and Ozzie with the World Series trophy

/// I didn't do anything. I'm not a magician.
I had great communication with the players.
But I also cause a lot of trouble for my players—
they have to deal with all the questions
about the things I'm saying all the time.

It was a tough season for us all. They trust me,
and I trust them. We're here together.
We play for one reason, and that's to win,
or lose, together. My players are the best
fighters anywhere. They stick together. The unity
of this team was great. We always feel we can
win because we're all pulling for each other
at the same time. ///

The celebration honoring the White Sox as World Series champions drew 2 million fans, purported to be the largest outdoor gathering in Chicago's history. While cheers rang out for even the most minor players, no ovations were louder than the applause showered down on Ozzie, who announced once and for all that, yes, he would return to manage in 2006.

/// I've been in a couple of parades and a couple of World Series, but these are the best fans I've ever seen, in the streets today in Chicago. I'm just excited for the people here. The people waited so long for this thing to happen, and believe me, it's something real nice.

I didn't come here for the glamour or the money. I came here to win. So it's a great feeling, what's happening right now. Finally, we do something for the [older] fans. They have been supporting this ballclub for so many years. They had waited so long. Thank you for the patience. Enjoy this. //

## chapter 13

# Aftermath/
# Looking Ahead

At the end of the season, the Baseball Writers' Association of America voted for their American and National League Managers of the Year. Predictably, Guillen was voted AL Manager of the Year with 17 first-place votes, five seconds, and five thirds. For the second straight season, Bobby Cox of the Atlanta Braves was the NL winner.

Afterward, Guillen again de-emphasized his own skills and elevated those of his players.

*// It's not easy to manage right now because there are a lot of players making big money, a lot of players with attitudes. The type of players I have in my clubhouse, those are the types of players anyone can win with.*

*We don't have superstars. We have guys who worry about the name on the chest more than the name on the back of the uniform. //*

After threatening earlier in the season to retire if the White Sox went all the way and won the World Series, Guillen rededicated himself to the pursuit at the end of the season, drawing upon a very famous former teammate.

*// I want to be like Michael Jordan,
have rings all over the place. //*

But naturally, the toll the long White Sox season took on Guillen—whose hair, curiously enough, never strayed from the jet-black of his rookie season—was never far from his mind.

*// The only bad thing about this was, we won a lot of
games by one run or two runs, and that drives me crazy. //*

From a managing standpoint, Guillen points to Cox as one of his biggest mentors. Guillen played under Cox in 1999 and made his only World Series appearance as a player with the Atlanta Braves.

*// There's nothing better than to be around
that man because he will teach you how to handle
things on the field and off the field. //*

For his part, Cox was delighted that the two men were honored in the same season.

**Cox:** He did a super, splendid job. I thought he was the right guy for that job.

Guillen admitted that his talk of retiring was a little silly. Cox, a baseball lifer, was one of the people who contacted him to tell him so.

**Cox:** Ozzie made his statement about retiring, and I couldn't believe it. We talked during the World Series and I told him that he was too good a man, too good a baseball man, to retire. We need people like him in baseball.

**Guillen:** I told him, "Skip, I already signed my contract"—but that wasn't good enough for him.

**Cox:** I said he needs to make them renew the contract now. Make them fire you. Keep taking the money away from them. Don't ever leave it on the table.

In November Ozzie fulfilled his promise to the people of Venezuela by bringing the 2005 World Series trophy to his homeland. It marked the first time in history that the award had left North America.

It was in Caracas that Guillen officially and completely reversed course from earlier talk of retirement by revealing a new managerial goal.

*// I have 10 fingers. I hope to fill them with rings. That's the motivation I have now. We are going to see results next year from what we're doing now, restructuring, working harder, investing money better to give the fans the feeling that this was not a one-time thing. //*

And, now that he's a World Series champion, will he be renegotiating his contract?

*// When a man signs a contract, he should honor it. They signed me for three seasons to win. They were going to pay me just the same, whether or not we were champions. The only thing that's changed is that my kids eat and drink for free in Chicago now. //*

One thing that will forever remain in Ozzie's methods will be his sense of fair play, treating his players equally, and doing so without fear.

*// I'll do it that way for the rest of my life. When a manager starts to lose his players, that manager deserves to be fired.*

*I don't care if I get fired. I have a lot of money. If I get fired, I'll get another job the next day. The very next day, I'll be wearing someone else's jersey. //*

# Appendix

## Ozzie Guillen's Major League Career

Oswaldo Jose Guillen Barrios

Bats: Left

Throws: Right

Height: 5'11"

Weight: 150 pounds

Born: January 20, 1964, in Ocumare del Tuy, Venezuela

Debut: April 9, 1985

Final Game: October 1, 2000

Shortstop 1985–2000: White Sox, Orioles, Braves, Devil Rays

Signed by the San Diego Padres as an amateur free agent in 1980.

All-Star in 1988, 1990, 1991

# Batting

| Year | Tm | G | AB | R | H | 2B | 3B | HR | RBI | SB | CS | BB | SO | BA | OBP | SLG | TB | SH | SF | IBB | HBP | GDP |
|---|---|---|---|---|---|---|---|---|---|---|---|---|---|---|---|---|---|---|---|---|---|---|
| 1985 | CHW | 150 | 491 | 71 | 134 | 21 | 9 | 1 | 33 | 7 | 4 | 12 | 36 | .273 | .291 | .358 | 176 | 8 | 1 | 1 | 1 | 5 |
| 1986 | CHW | 159 | 547 | 58 | 137 | 19 | 2 | 2 | 47 | 8 | 4 | 12 | 52 | .250 | .265 | .311 | 170 | 12 | 5 | 1 | 1 | 14 |
| 1987 | CHW | 149 | 560 | 64 | 156 | 22 | 7 | 2 | 51 | 25 | 8 | 22 | 52 | .279 | .303 | .354 | 198 | 13 | 8 | 2 | 1 | 10 |
| 1988 | CHW | 156 | 566 | 58 | 148 | 16 | 7 | 0 | 39 | 25 | 13 | 25 | 40 | .261 | .294 | .314 | 178 | 10 | 3 | 3 | 2 | 14 |
| 1989 | CHW | 155 | 597 | 63 | 151 | 20 | 8 | 1 | 54 | 36 | 17 | 15 | 48 | .253 | .270 | .318 | 190 | 11 | 3 | 3 | 0 | 8 |
| 1990 | CHW | 160 | 516 | 61 | 144 | 21 | 4 | 1 | 58 | 13 | 17 | 26 | 37 | .279 | .312 | .341 | 176 | 15 | 5 | 8 | 1 | 6 |
| 1991 | CHW | 154 | 524 | 52 | 143 | 20 | 3 | 3 | 49 | 21 | 15 | 11 | 38 | .273 | .284 | .340 | 178 | 13 | 7 | 1 | 0 | 7 |
| 1992 | CHW | 12 | 40 | 5 | 8 | 4 | 0 | 0 | 7 | 1 | 0 | 1 | 5 | .200 | .214 | .300 | 12 | 1 | 1 | 0 | 0 | 1 |
| 1993 | CHW | 134 | 457 | 44 | 128 | 23 | 4 | 4 | 50 | 5 | 5 | 10 | 41 | .280 | .292 | .374 | 171 | 13 | 6 | 0 | 0 | 6 |
| 1994 | CHW | 100 | 365 | 46 | 105 | 9 | 5 | 1 | 39 | 5 | 4 | 14 | 35 | .288 | .311 | .348 | 127 | 7 | 4 | 2 | 0 | 5 |
| 1995 | CHW | 122 | 415 | 50 | 103 | 20 | 3 | 1 | 41 | 6 | 7 | 13 | 25 | .248 | .270 | .318 | 132 | 4 | 1 | 1 | 0 | 11 |
| 1996 | CHW | 150 | 499 | 62 | 131 | 24 | 8 | 4 | 45 | 6 | 5 | 10 | 27 | .263 | .273 | .367 | 183 | 12 | 7 | 0 | 0 | 10 |
| 1997 | CHW | 142 | 490 | 59 | 120 | 21 | 6 | 4 | 52 | 5 | 3 | 22 | 24 | .245 | .275 | .337 | 165 | 11 | 4 | 1 | 0 | 7 |
| 1998 | BAL | 12 | 16 | 2 | 1 | 0 | 0 | 0 | 0 | 0 | 1 | 1 | 2 | .062 | .118 | .062 | 1 | 1 | 0 | 0 | 0 | 2 |
| 1998 | ATL | 83 | 264 | 35 | 73 | 15 | 1 | 1 | 22 | 1 | 4 | 24 | 25 | .277 | .337 | .352 | 93 | 4 | 2 | 0 | 1 | 2 |
| 1998 | TOT | 95 | 280 | 37 | 74 | 15 | 1 | 1 | 22 | 1 | 5 | 25 | 27 | .264 | .325 | .336 | 94 | 5 | 2 | 0 | 1 | 3 |
| 1999 | ATL | 92 | 232 | 21 | 56 | 16 | 0 | 1 | 20 | 4 | 2 | 15 | 17 | .241 | .284 | .323 | 75 | 5 | 3 | 2 | 0 | 6 |
| 2000 | TBD | 63 | 107 | 22 | 26 | 4 | 0 | 2 | 12 | 1 | 0 | 6 | 7 | .243 | .283 | .336 | 36 | 1 | 0 | 0 | 0 | 1 |
| 16 Seasons | | 1993 | 6686 | 773 | 1764 | 275 | 69 | 28 | 619 | 169 | 108 | 239 | 511 | .264 | .287 | .338 | 141 | 60 | 25 | 7 | 1 | 14 |
| 162 Game Avg | | | 543 | 63 | 143 | 22 | 6 | 2 | 50 | 14 | 9 | 19 | 42 | .264 | .287 | .338 | 184 | 11 | 5 | 2 | 1 | 9 |
| Career High | | 160 | 597 | 71 | 156 | 24 | 9 | 4 | 58 | 36 | 17 | 26 | 52 | .288 | .325 | .374 | 198 | 15 | 8 | 8 | 2 | 14 |

# Fielding

| Year | Tm | Pos | G | PO | A | E | DP | FP | League FP |
|------|-----|-----|------|------|------|-----|------|-------|-----------|
| 1985 | CHW | SS | 150 | 220 | 382 | 12 | 80 | .980 | .964 |
| 1986 | CHW | SS | 157 | 261 | 459 | 22 | 93 | .970 | .967 |
| | | DH | 1 | | | | | | |
| 1987 | CHW | SS | 149 | 266 | 475 | 19 | 105 | .975 | .970 |
| 1988 | CHW | SS | 156 | 273 | 570 | 20 | 115 | .977 | .971 |
| 1989 | CHW | SS | 155 | 272 | 512 | 22 | 106 | .973 | .971 |
| 1990 | CHW | SS | 159 | 252 | 474 | 17 | 100 | .977 | .973 |
| 1991 | CHW | SS | 149 | 249 | 439 | 21 | 88 | .970 | .971 |
| 1992 | CHW | SS | 12 | 20 | 39 | 0 | 7 | 1.000 | .969 |
| 1993 | CHW | SS | 133 | 189 | 361 | 16 | 82 | .972 | .973 |
| 1994 | CHW | SS | 99 | 139 | 237 | 16 | 46 | .959 | .969 |
| 1995 | CHW | SS | 120 | 167 | 318 | 12 | 58 | .976 | .974 |
| | | DH | 1 | | | | | | |
| 1996 | CHW | SS | 146 | 220 | 348 | 11 | 69 | .981 | .971 |
| | | LF | 2 | 2 | 0 | 0 | 0 | 1.000 | .979 |
| 1997 | CHW | SS | 139 | 207 | 348 | 15 | 78 | .974 | .974 |
| 1998 | BAL | SS | 6 | 3 | 11 | 1 | 1 | .933 | .972 |
| | | 3B | 1 | 0 | 0 | 0 | 0 | | |
| | ATL | SS | 71 | 93 | 160 | 6 | 25 | .977 | .968 |
| | | 2B | 2 | 1 | 5 | 0 | 1 | 1.000 | .982 |
| | | 1B | 1 | 2 | 0 | 0 | 0 | 1.000 | .993 |
| | | 3B | 1 | 1 | 1 | 0 | 0 | 1.000 | .957 |
| | TOT | SS | 77 | 96 | 171 | 7 | 26 | .974 | .968 |
| | TOT | 3B | 2 | 1 | 1 | 0 | 0 | 1.000 | .952 |
| 1999 | ATL | SS | 53 | 54 | 137 | 7 | 29 | .965 | .967 |
| | | 3B | 6 | 3 | 9 | 0 | 1 | 1.000 | .953 |
| | | 2B | 1 | 1 | 0 | 0 | 0 | 1.000 | .981 |
| 2000 | TBD | SS | 42 | 26 | 65 | 5 | 12 | .948 | .973 |
| | | 3B | 11 | 4 | 22 | 0 | 2 | 1.000 | .947 |
| | | 1B | 5 | 7 | 1 | 0 | 0 | 1.000 | .993 |
| | | 2B | 2 | 3 | 2 | 0 | 0 | 1.000 | .980 |
| Position Total | | SS | 1896 | 2911 | 5335 | 222 | 1094 | .974 | .970 |
| | | 3B | 19 | 8 | 32 | 0 | 3 | 1.000 | .949 |
| | | 1B | 6 | 9 | 1 | 0 | 0 | 1.000 | .993 |
| | | 2B | 5 | 5 | 7 | 0 | 1 | 1.000 | .981 |
| | | DH | 2 | Games not counted in Overall Total below | | | | | |
| | | LF | 2 | 2 | 0 | 0 | 0 | 1.000 | .979 |
| Overall Total | | | 1928 | 2935 | 5375 | 222 | 1098 | .974 | .970 |

# Postseason Batting

| Year | Round | Tm | Opp | W/L | G | AB | R | H | 2B | 3B | HR | RBI | BB | SO | BA | OBP | SLG | SB | CS | SH | SF | HBP |
|------|-------|-----|-----|-----|----|----|---|----|----|----|----|-----|----|----|------|------|------|----|----|----|----|-----|
| 1993 | ALCS | CHW | TOR | L | 6 | 22 | 4 | 6 | 1 | 0 | 0 | 2 | 0 | 2 | .273 | .273 | .318 | 1 | 0 | 1 | 0 | 0 |
| 1998 | NLDS | ATL | CHC | W | 1 | 1 | 0 | 0 | 0 | 0 | 0 | 0 | 0 | 0 | .000 | .000 | .000 | 0 | 0 | 0 | 0 | 0 |
|      | NLCS | ATL | SDP | L | 4 | 12 | 1 | 5 | 0 | 0 | 0 | 1 | 0 | 1 | .417 | .417 | .417 | 0 | 0 | 0 | 0 | 0 |
| 1999 | NLDS | ATL | HOU | W | 1 | 1 | 0 | 0 | 0 | 0 | 0 | 0 | 0 | 0 | .000 | .000 | .000 | 0 | 0 | 0 | 0 | 0 |
|      | NLCS | ATL | NYM | W | 3 | 3 | 0 | 1 | 0 | 0 | 0 | 1 | 0 | 1 | .333 | .333 | .333 | 0 | 0 | 0 | 0 | 0 |
|      | WS | ATL | NYY | L | 3 | 5 | 0 | 0 | 0 | 0 | 0 | 0 | 0 | 0 | .000 | .000 | .000 | 0 | 0 | 0 | 0 | 0 |
| 2 LDS | | | | 2-0 | 2 | 2 | 0 | 0 | 0 | 0 | 0 | 0 | 0 | 0 | .000 | .000 | .000 | 0 | 0 | 0 | 0 | 0 |
| 3 LCS | | | | 1-2 | 13 | 37 | 5 | 12 | 1 | 0 | 0 | 4 | 0 | 3 | .324 | .324 | .351 | 1 | 0 | 1 | 0 | 0 |
| 6 Total Postseasons | | | | 3-3 | 18 | 44 | 5 | 12 | 1 | 0 | 0 | 4 | 0 | 4 | .273 | .273 | .295 | 1 | 0 | 1 | 0 | 0 |

# Leaderboards and Awards

Awards are Year-League-Award, Stats are Year-Value-Rank

| All-Star | Awards | Gold Gloves | MVP | Games | Triples |
|----------|--------|-------------|-----|-------|---------|
| 1988 | 1985-AL-ROY | 1990-AL—SS | (Yr-Lg-Rk-Shares) | 1986-159-9 | 1985-9-5 |
| 1990 | | | 1990-AL-17-0.03 | 1990-160-4 | 1987-7-9 |
| 1991 | | | Car-1170-0.03 | | 1988-7-5 |
| | | | shares | | 1989-8-8 |
| | | | | | 1994-5-8 |
| | | | | | 1996-8-3 |
| | | | | | 1997-6-10 |

| Stolen Bases | Singles | Sac. Hits | Sac. Flies | At-Bats per Strikeout |
|--------------|---------|-----------|------------|-----------------------|
| 1989-36-7 | 1987-125-10 | 1986-12-6 | 1987-8-8 | 1985-13.6-7 |
| | 1994-90-8 | 1987-13-6 | | 1986-10.5-9 |
| | | 1990-15-3 | | 1988-14.2-8 |
| | | 1991-13-4 | | 1989-12.4-8 |
| | | 1993-13-4 | | 1990-13.9-3 |
| | | 1994-7-10 | | 1991-13.8-9 |
| | | 1996-12-7 | | 1994-10.4-9 |
| | | 1997-11-4 | | 1995-**16.6-8 |
| | | | | 1996-18.5-1 |
| | | | | 1997-20.4-1 |

A ** by the stat's value indicates the player had fewer than the required number of at-bats or plate appearances for the BA, OBP, SLG, or OPS title that year. In order to rank the player, the necessary number of hitless at-bats were added to the player's season total. The value printed here is their actual value and not the value used to rank them, therefore some numbers may appear out of order. Requirements to qualify for rate stats.

# Managerial Record

| Year | League | Team | Age | G | W | L | WP | Finish |
|------|--------|------|-----|-----|-----|-----|------|--------|
| 2004 | AL Cent | CHW | 40 | 162 | 83 | 79 | .512 | 2 |
| 2005 | AL Cent | CHW | 41 | 162 | 99 | 63 | .611 | 1 |
| TOTAL | | | | 324 | 182 | 142 | .562 | |

# Venezuelan Players in the Majors

Between 1939 and 2005, 181 players from Venezuela had appeared in the major leagues. Ozzie Guillen's hero, Chico Carrasquel, was the third Venezuelan major leaguer. Luis Aparicio, whose uncle tutored Guillen in Venezuela, was the sixth. Ozzie himself was the 36th. All three shortstops made their debuts with the Chicago White Sox. A-S denotes All-Star player.

| No | Name | Pos | Team | Date of Debut |
|----|------|-----|------|---------------|
| 1 | Alex Carrasquel | P | Washington Senators | April 23, 1939 |
| 2 | Chucho Ramos | OF | Cincinnati Reds | May 7, 1944 |
| 3 | Chico Carrasquel A-S | SS | Chicago White Sox | April 18, 1950 |
| 4 | Pompeyo Davalillo | SS | Washington Senators | August 1, 1953 |
| 5 | Ramon Monzant | P | New York Giants | July 2, 1954 |
| 6 | Luis Aparicio HOF | SS | Chicago White Sox | April 17, 1956 |
| 7 | Elio Chacon | 2B | Cincinnati Reds | April 20, 1960 |
| 8 | Víctor Davalillo A-S | OF | Cleveland Indians | April 9, 1963 |
| 9 | Cesar Tovar | IF | Minnesota Twins | April 12, 1965 |
| 10 | Gustavo Gil | 2B | Cleveland Indians | April 11, 1967 |
| 11 | Cesar Gutierrez | SS | San Francisco Giants | April 16, 1967 |
| 12 | Roberto Rodríguez | P | Kansas City Athletics | May 13, 1967 |
| 13 | Jose Herrera | OF | Houston Astros | June 3, 1967 |
| 14 | Nestor Chavez | P | San Francisco Giants | September 9, 1967 |
| 15 | Remigio Hermoso | SS | Atlanta Braves | September 14, 1967 |
| 16 | Angel Bravo | OF | Chicago White Sox | June 6, 1969 |
| 17 | Dave Concepcion A-S | SS | Cincinnati Reds | April 6, 1970 |
| 18 | Oswaldo Blanco | 1B | Chicago White Sox | May 26, 1970 |
| 19 | Enzo Hernandez | SS | San Diego Padres | April 17, 1971 |

| 20 | Damaso Blanco | SS | San Francisco Giants | May 26, 1972 |
| 21 | Gonzalo Márquez | 1B | Oakland Athletics | August 11, 1972 |
| 22 | Manny Trillo A-S | 2B | Oakland Athletics | June 28, 1973 |
| 23 | Pablo Torrealba | P | Atlanta Braves | April 9, 1975 |
| 24 | Manny Sarmiento | P | Cincinnati Reds | July 30, 1976 |
| 25 | Tony Armas A-S | OF | Pittsburgh Pirates | September 6, 1976 |
| 26 | Bo Díaz A-S | C | Boston Red Sox | September 6, 1977 |
| 27 | Luis Leal | P | Toronto Blue Jays | May 25, 1980 |
| 28 | Luis Salazar | 3B | San Diego Padres | August 15, 1980 |
| 29 | Luis Aponte | P | Boston Red Sox | September 4, 1980 |
| 30 | Luis Sanchez | P | California Angels | April 10, 1981 |
| 31 | Fred Manrique | 2B | Toronto Blue Jays | August 23, 1981 |
| 32 | Leonardo Hernandez | 3B | Baltimore Orioles | August 19, 1982 |
| 33 | Argenis Salazar | SS | Montreal Expos | August 10, 1983 |
| 34 | Tobias Hernandez | C | Toronto Blue Jays | June 22, 1984 |
| 35 | Alvaro Espinoza | SS | Minnesota Twins | September 14, 1984 |
| 36 | Ozzie Guillen A-S | SS | Chicago White Sox | April 9, 1985 |
| 37 | Urbano Lugo | P | California Angels | April 28, 1985 |
| 38 | Andres Galarraga A-S | 1B | Montreal Expos | August 23, 1985 |
| 39 | Gustavo Polidor | SS | California Angels | September 7, 1985 |
| 40 | Lester Straker | P | Minnesota Twins | April 11, 1987 |
| 41 | Al Pedrique | SS | New York Mets | April 14, 1987 |
| 42 | Miguel Angel García | P | California Angels | April 30, 1987 |
| 43 | Ubaldo Heredia | P | Montreal Expos | May 12, 1987 |
| 44 | Alexis Infante | IF | Toronto Blue Jays | September 27, 1987 |
| 45 | Oswaldo Peraza | P | Baltimore Orioles | April 4, 1988 |
| 46 | Johnny Paredes | 2B | Montreal Expos | April 29, 1988 |
| 47 | Angel Escobar | IF | San Francisco Giants | May 17, 1988 |
| 48 | German Gonzalez | P | Minnesota Twins | August 5, 1988 |
| 49 | Antonio Castillo | P | Toronto Blue Jays | August 14, 1988 |
| 50 | Carlos Martínez | 3B | Chicago White Sox | September 2, 1988 |
| 51 | Carlos Quintana | 1B | Boston Red Sox | September 16, 1988 |
| 52 | Omar Vizquel A-S | SS | Seattle Mariners | April 3, 1989 |

| 53 | Wilson Alvarez | P | Texas Rangers | July 24, 1989 |
| 54 | Julio Machado | P | New York Mets | September 7, 1989 |
| 55 | Carlos A. Hernandez | C | Los Angeles Dodgers | April 20, 1990 |
| 56 | Luis Sojo | 2B | Toronto Blue Jays | July 14, 1990 |
| 57 | Oscar Azocar | OF | New York Yankees | July 17, 1990 |
| 58 | Rich Garces | P | Minnesota Twins | September 18, 1990 |
| 59 | Carlos Garcia A-S | 2B | Pittsburgh Pirates | September 20, 1990 |
| 60 | Jose Escobar | SS | Cleveland Indians | April 13, 1991 |
| 61 | Ramon García | P | Chicago White Sox | May 31, 1991 |
| 62 | Amalio Carreno | P | Philadelphia Phillies | July 7, 1991 |
| 63 | Danilo Leon | P | Texas Rangers | June 6, 1992 |
| 64 | Cristobal Colon | SS | Texas Rangers | September 18, 1992 |
| 65 | William Canate | OF | Toronto Blue Jays | April 16, 1993 |
| 66 | Omar Daal | P | Los Angeles Dodgers | April 23, 1993 |
| 67 | Marcos Armas | OF | Oakland Athletics | May 25, 1993 |
| 68 | Pedro Castellano | 3B | Colorado Rockies | May 30, 1993 |
| 69 | Eduardo Zambrano | 1B | Chicago Cubs | September 19, 1993 |
| 70 | Roberto Petagine | 1B | Houston Astros | April 4, 1994 |
| 71 | Juan Carlos Pulido | P | Minnesota Twins | April 9, 1994 |
| 72 | Robert Perez | OF | Toronto Blue Jays | July 20, 1994 |
| 73 | Juan Castillo | P | New York Mets | July 26, 1994 |
| 74 | Edgardo Alfonzo A-S | 2B | New York Mets | April 26, 1995 |
| 75 | Felipe Lira | P | Detroit Tigers | April 27, 1995 |
| 76 | Dilson Torres | P | Kansas City Royals | April 29, 1995 |
| 77 | Tomás Perez | 2B | Toronto Blue Jays | May 3, 1995 |
| 78 | Ugueth Urbina A-S | P | Montreal Expos | May 9, 1995 |
| 79 | Edwin Hurtado | P | Toronto Blue Jays | May 22, 1995 |
| 80 | Edgar Caceres | 2B | Kansas City Royals | June 8, 1995 |
| 81 | Roger Cedeno | OF | Los Angeles Dodgers | June 20, 1995 |
| 82 | Giovanni Carrara | P | Toronto Blue Jays | July 29, 1995 |
| 83 | Eddie Perez | C | Atlanta Braves | August 10, 1995 |
| 84 | Alex Delgado | C | Boston Red Sox | April 4, 1996 |
| 85 | Alex Pacheco | P | Montreal Expos | April 17, 1996 |

| 86 | Miguel Cairo | 2B | Toronto Blue Jays | April 17, 1996 |
| 87 | Jose Malave | OF | Boston Red Sox | May 23, 1996 |
| 88 | Robert Machado | C | Chicago White Sox | July 24, 1996 |
| 89 | Raul Chavez | C | Montreal Expos | August 30, 1996 |
| 90 | Bobby Abreu A-S | RF | Houston Astros | September 1, 1996 |
| 91 | Eddy Díaz | 2B | Milwaukee Brewers | April 17, 1997 |
| 92 | Edgar Ramos | P | Philadelphia Phillies | May 5, 1997 |
| 93 | Jeremi Gonzalez | P | Chicago Cubs | May 27, 1997 |
| 94 | Jorge Velandia | SS | San Diego Padres | June 20, 1997 |
| 95 | Kelvim Escobar | P | Toronto Blue Jays | June 29, 1997 |
| 96 | Henry Blanco | C | Los Angeles Dodgers | July 25, 1997 |
| 97 | Magglio Ordonez A-S | RF | Chicago White Sox | August 29, 1997 |
| 98 | Richard Hidalgo | OF | Houston Astros | September 1, 1997 |
| 99 | Luis Ordaz | SS | St. Louis Cardinals | September 3, 1997 |
| 100 | Carlos Mendoza | OF | New York Mets | September 3, 1997 |
| 101 | Oscar Henriquez | P | Houston Astros | September 7, 1997 |
| 102 | Giomar Guevara | SS | Seattle Mariners | September 19, 1997 |
| 103 | Jose Miguel Nieves | IF | Chicago Cubs | August 7, 1998 |
| 104 | Alex Gonzalez A-S | SS | Florida Marlins | August 25, 1998 |
| 105 | Carlos Guillen A-S | SS | Seattle Mariners | September 6, 1998 |
| 106 | Alex Ramirez | OF | Cleveland Indians | September 19, 1998 |
| 107 | Freddy Garcia A-S | P | Seattle Mariners | April 7, 1999 |
| 108 | Beiker Graterol | P | Detroit Tigers | April 9, 1999 |
| 109 | Horacio Estrada | P | Milwaukee Brewers | May 4, 1999 |
| 110 | Orber Moreno | P | Kansas City Royals | May 25, 1999 |
| 111 | Carlos Hernandez | 2B | Houston Astros | May 26, 1999 |
| 112 | Melvin Mora A-S | OF | New York Mets | May 30, 1999 |
| 113 | Liu Rodriguez | 2B | Chicago White Sox | June 9, 1999 |
| 114 | Ramon Hernandez A-S | C | Oakland Athletics | June 29, 1999 |
| 115 | Wiki Gonzalez | C | San Diego Padres | August 14, 1999 |
| 116 | Tony Armas, Jr. | P | Montreal Expos | August 16, 1999 |
| 117 | Johan Santana A-S | P | Minnesota Twins | April 3, 2000 |

| 118 | Ruben Quevedo | P | Chicago Cubs | April 14, 2000 |
| 119 | Fernando Lunar | C | Atlanta Braves | May 8, 2000 |
| 120 | Darwin Cubillan | P | Toronto Blue Jays | May 20, 2000 |
| 121 | William Martinez | P | Cleveland Indians | June 14, 2000 |
| 122 | Alex Cabrera | 1B | Arizona Diamondbacks | June 26, 2000 |
| 123 | Luis Rivas | 2B | Minnesota Twins | September 16, 2000 |
| 124 | Clemente Alvarez | C | Philadelphia Phillies | September 19, 2000 |
| 125 | Donaldo Mendez | SS | San Diego Padres | April 5, 2001 |
| 126 | Jorge Julio Tapia | P | Baltimore Orioles | April 26, 2001 |
| 127 | Alex Escobar | OF | New York Mets | May 8, 2001 |
| 128 | Juan Moreno | P | Texas Rangers | May 17, 2001 |
| 129 | Endy Chavez | OF | Kansas City Royals | May 29, 2001 |
| 130 | Juan Rincon | P | Minnesota Twins | June 7, 2001 |
| 131 | Victor Zambrano | P | Tampa Bay Devil Rays | June 21, 2001 |
| 132 | Cesar Izturis A-S | SS | Toronto Blue Jays | June 23, 1999 |
| 133 | Carlos E. Hernandez | P | Houston Astros | August 8, 2001 |
| 134 | Carlos Zambrano A-S | P | Chicago Cubs | August 20, 2001 |
| 135 | Juan Rivera | OF | New York Yankees | September 4, 2001 |
| 136 | Yorvit Torrealba | C | San Francisco Giants | September 5, 2001 |
| 137 | Wilfredo Rodriguez | P | Houston Astros | September 21, 2001 |
| 138 | Steve Torrealba | C | Atlanta Braves | October 6, 2001 |
| 139 | Carlos Silva | P | Philadelphia Phillies | April 1, 2002 |
| 140 | Luis Ugueto | SS | Seattle Mariners | April 3, 2002 |
| 141 | Felix Escalona | SS | Tampa Bay Devil Rays | April 4, 2002 |
| 142 | Oscar Salazar | 2B | Detroit Tigers | April 10, 2002 |
| 143 | Marco Scutaro | 2B | New York Mets | July 21, 2002 |
| 144 | Antonio Alvarez | OF | Pittsburgh Pirates | September 4, 2002 |
| 145 | Omar Infante | SS | Detroit Tigers | September 7, 2002 |
| 146 | Víctor Martinez A-S | C | Cleveland Indians | September 10, 2002 |
| 147 | Alex Herrera | P | Cleveland Indians | September 13, 2002 |
| 148 | Frankie Rodriguez A-S | P | Anaheim Angels | September 18, 2002 |
| 149 | Wilfredo Ledezma | P | Detroit Tigers | April 2, 2003 |
| 150 | Rosman Garcia | P | Texas Rangers | April 19, 2003 |

| 151 | Carlos Mendez | C | Baltimore Orioles | May 22, 2003 |
| 152 | Ray Olmedo | SS | Cincinnati Reds | May 25, 2003 |
| 153 | Miguel Cabrera A-S | OF | Florida Marlins | June 20, 2003 |
| 154 | Carlos Valderrama | OF | San Francisco Giants | June 21, 2003 |
| 155 | Rafael Betancourt | P | Cleveland Indians | July 13, 2003 |
| 156 | Rene Reyes | OF | Colorado Rockies | July 22, 2003 |
| 157 | Alex Prieto | 2B | Minnesota Twins | July 26, 2003 |
| 158 | Humberto Quintero | C | San Diego Padres | September 3, 2003 |
| 159 | Anderson Machado | SS | Philadelphia Phillies | September 27, 2003 |
| 160 | Luis A. Gonzalez | 2B | Colorado Rockies | April 6, 2004 |
| 161 | Jose Castillo | 2B | Pittsburgh Pirates | April 7, 2004 |
| 162 | Andres Blanco | SS | Kansas City Royals | April 18, 2004 |
| 163 | Eduardo Villacis | P | Kansas City Royals | May 2, 2004 |
| 164 | Ramon A. Castro | SS | Oakland Athletics | June 21, 2004 |
| 165 | Jose Lopez | SS | Seattle Mariners | July 31, 2004 |
| 166 | Maicer Izturis | SS | Montreal Expos | August 27, 2004 |
| 167 | Guillermo Quiroz | C | Toronto Blue Jays | September 4, 2004 |
| 168 | Dioner Navarro | C | New York Yankees | September 7, 2004 |
| 169 | Lino Urdaneta | P | Detroit Tigers | September 9, 2004 |
| 170 | Gustavo Chacin | P | Toronto Blue Jays | September 20, 2004 |
| 171 | Marcos Carvajal | P | Colorado Rockies | April 6, 2005 |
| 172 | Ronny Cedeno | SS | Chicago Cubs | April 23, 2005 |
| 173 | William Bergolla | 2B | Cincinnati Reds | May 9, 2005 |
| 174 | Luis Rodriguez | SS | Minnesota Twins | May 21, 2005 |
| 175 | Yorman Bazardo | P | Florida Marlins | May 26, 2005 |
| 176 | Danny Sandoval | SS | Philadelphia Phillies | July 17, 2005 |
| 177 | Felix Hernandez | P | Seattle Mariners | August 4, 2005 |
| 178 | Alejandro Freire | 1B | Baltimore Orioles | August 9, 2005 |
| 179 | Franklin Gutierrez | OF | Cleveland Indians | August 31, 2005 |
| 180 | Alejandro Machado | 2B | Boston Red Sox | September 3, 2005 |
| 181 | Miguel Perez | C | Cincinnati Reds | September 7, 2005 |

# Notes

## Chapter 1

1. Ed Sherman, "What if...the Sox hadn't traded for Ozzie: White Sox GM Roland Hemond bucked popular opinion in trading for the San Diego minor-leaguer in 1984," *Chicago Tribune*, October 10, 2005
2. Phil Rogers, "After 13 years, Guillen's 'sad' day arrives," *Chicago Tribune*, September 26, 1997
3. Marc Topkin, "Guillen weighs options, particularly retirement," *St. Petersburg Times*, April 2, 2001

## Chapter 2

4. "White Sox name Ozzie Guillen manager," *Sportsticker*, November 3, 2003

## Chapter 3

5. Scott Merkin, "Stunning Shingo," *Whitesox.com (http://www.mlb.com/NASApp/mlb/cws/news/cws_news.jsp?),* February 21, 2004
6. Ozzie Guillen, "Closer," *El Universal,* April 4, 2004
7. Rick Morrissey, "Hugs for all: Guillen's debut ends happily," *Chicago Tribune,* April 14, 2004

8. John Weyler, "Showalter sets off Guillen," *Chicago Tribune*, September 12, 2004

## Chapter 4

9. Ozzie Guillen, "El Chico," *El Universal*, May 28, 2005
10. "Venezuelan president congratulates Guillen on World Series victory," *Associated Press*, October 30, 2005

## Chapter 5

11. Ozzie Guillen, "Rivalries," *El Universal*, May 21, 2005

## Chapter 6

12. Ozzie Guillen, "Starting the season," *El Universal*, April 23, 2005
13. Ozzie Guillen, "To Third," *El Universal*, April 16, 2005
14. Ozzie Guillen, "Luck," *El Universal*, June 11, 2005
15. Ozzie Guillen, "Critics," *El Universal*, June 18, 2005
16. Ozzie Guillen, "It is the truth," *El Universal*, October 1, 2005

## Chapter 11

17. Michael Farber, "Living out loud: He may not be politically correct, but the often unconventional and always outspoken Ozzie Guillen has made the South Side exciting again," *Sports Illustrated*, World Series Commemorative Edition 2005, pp. 11–17
18. "White Sox name Ozzie Guillen manager," *Sportsticker*, November 3, 2003

## Appendix

Career Statistics: *www.baseball-reference.com*
*(http://www.baseball-reference.com/g/guilloz01.shtml)*

# Photo Credits

**Page 3:** National Baseball Hall of Fame Library, Cooperstown, N.Y.

**Page 4:** AP/Wide World Photos

**Page 21:** Getty Images

**Page 28:** Getty Images

**Page 52:** AP/Wide World Photos

**Page 55:** AP/Wide World Photos

**Page 61:** AP/Wide World Photos

**Page 64:** AP/Wide World Photos

**Page 69:** Getty Images

**Page 85:** AP/Wide World Photos

**Page 89:** Getty Images